Colors *of the* Spirit

Colors *of the* Spirit

Dorothy K. Ederer

Doubleday

New York London Toronto Sydney Auckland

Published by Doubleday
a division of Bantam Doubleday Dell Publishing Group, Inc.
1540 Broadway, New York, New York 10036

DOUBLEDAY and the portrayal of an anchor with a dolphin
are trademarks of Doubleday, a division of Bantam
Doubleday Dell Publishing Group, Inc.

Book design by Jennifer Ann Daddio

Library of Congress Cataloging-in-Publication Data
Ederer, Dorothy K.
Colors of the spirit / Dorothy K. Ederer.—1st ed.
p.   cm.
1. Christian life—Catholic authors.   I. Title.
BX2350.2.E334   1998
248.4—dc21   98-13271
CIP

ISBN 0-385-48848-3
Copyright © 1998 by Dorothy K. Ederer
All Rights Reserved
Printed in the United States of America
September 1998
First Edition
1 3 5 7 9 10 8 6 4 2

I dedicate this book to my parents,

Ann and Bernard Ederer,

who have also been my best friends.

I dedicate this book as well to my brothers,

Bernard and Father John,

and to my sisters,

Carol, Jeanne, Julie, and Geralyn.

Their loyalty and support have been

unwavering through happy and difficult times.

Acknowledgments

I could not have survived this manuscript without the patient guidance and whimsical suggestions of Joseph Girzone. His playful humor was always well timed. He has shown himself a true friend.

I want also to thank especially Pierrette Virkler, our secretary. She has been, in her quiet, dedicated way, an inestimable support.

I am grateful in a special way to Peter Ginsberg, my agent, whose faith at times seemed beyond reason, but whose encouragement has proven that we rise to the level of loved one's expectations.

Trace Murphy, my editor at Doubleday, has become a warm friend as well as a kind and gentle critic. My gratitude to Trace is deep and lasting.

Contents

Colors *of the* Spirit

Foreword

$\mathscr{T}$he longer I live, the simpler life appears. What is so difficult to understand is why human beings live in such unending conflict, and continually generate so many unresolvable problems. Of late, it dawned on me what appears to be the basis for the phenomenon: No two people see things in exactly the same way. To the simple question "How are you?" one person will respond with a grateful smile and a "Fine, thank you." "Why do you ask?" will be another person's response. A simple look of bewilderment will be a third person's reaction. "It's a nice day," a fourth will reply without answering the question. "Why do you ask? Don't I look well?" another might say. Some reactions can be downright hostile. Each person's response expresses the way he or she views the question, and his or her mood at the time. The same diversity of observations is seen when a number of people have witnessed the same event. You wonder if they all saw the same thing. It is almost as if each person has a different pair of glasses which focuses on different facets of the same object and biases the viewer. And then there's human nature. Some people are happy, some are melancholy. Others are suspicious and some absolutely paranoid. I have friends who always see the dark side. One day I gave a gold piece as a present to one of these friends. His first comment was "Oh, but what am I going to do with it? I'm sure I will lose it." So the next day he sold it. I was a little annoyed, because I had been saving it for years as part of an investment for my retirement. During the next two weeks the value of that gold piece went up forty dollars. I know it was only money, but the incident taught me a lesson about the different ways people perceive things.

My father was the type of person who seemed to have been born with a happy spirit and always saw things through rose-colored glasses. Even on dismal, rainy days he would remark, "What a beautiful day!" It used to annoy me, because if it was raining, I could not see anything good about it, especially if there was no school. But he did not make such remarks just to be contrary. He really felt it was a good day. Even during the most difficult times in his life he had that same attitude. For example, he and my mother had had nine children and he was drafted into the army. The news reporters came to the house and, after asking him how he felt about being drafted, asked him what would happen to his wife and the children if he should die. His answer was a shock. "If God can use *me* to take care of the family, He can do just as good a job without me."

I think people who enter the news industry have all been born with black glasses. They seem to have an obsession with the dark and sick side of life. I hardly read the newspapers anymore; they are too depressing. I think they are responsible for the depression and hopelessness so many people feel today. Just as a family would be torn apart if one member is depressed, the worldwide family is affected by the media's emphasis on the darker side of life.

Four years ago I met Sister Dorothy. I was immediately impressed with her extraordinarily happy spirit. Her rose-colored glasses were obvious. I do not think I ever met a person who found such simple, childlike joy in life. She reminded me of Whoopi Goldberg in *Sister Act*, and Maria in the *The Sound of Music* combined. In reading *Colors of the Spirit*, I felt Dorothy's happy spirit on every page. Her love of people and her ability to see good in people where others might see only evil is so healthy and uplifting, it was truly a joy for me to read this wonderful manuscript. I think our world needs that spirit if we are ever to rekindle a sense of joy and humor in the human family. We need the hope that that outlook can inspire. One grows weary of those who are offered a pile of diamonds and look for the speck of dirt that they seem to value more than the diamonds. In *Colors of the Spirit*, Dorothy Ederer looks across a worn-out humanity and finds priceless treasures. I hope that this literary endeavor is just the beginning of her writing career. The world needs her optimism and happy, childlike spirit. It is like a songbird's return at the end of a long, cold winter. I have no doubt that this little book will quietly find its way into the hearts of the many people who are looking for bright sunshine and spring flowers.

—JOSEPH F. GIRZONE

Introduction

*I*t doesn't matter if I pick up the newspaper, turn on the television, or listen to the radio, I am bombarded with stories about the dark side of people's lives. It seems that everything that happens throughout the world is based on endless conflict. Either it is the "crime of the century," a celebrity marriage falling apart, or the hatred that has divided people along ethnic lines in some distant (or not so distant) part of the world. Faced with all this, I can't help wondering whether the world is a sick place.

And yet I have never lost my faith in people. I have always believed that people were basically good, that in time everyone's good side would show. Maybe it is because I see people at their best so much that I found a reason for hope even in the darkest situations.

In the following pages I share with you real-life adventures. Some are my own, some are from the lives of people I have known over the years. I have been deeply touched by each of these incidents. You will see in these stories remarkable individuals who discovered the potential goodness lying within and also the striking effect their lives have had on others.

Merely witnessing these powerful experiences enriched my life. They have brightened the colors of my world, a world that is sometimes darkened by the pain and desperation I often encounter in those I meet. These individuals have been a sort of spiritual rainbow, each reflecting a different color with a unique meaning. For this reason I have chosen the rainbow as the vehicle for sharing these experiences, with each color having a certain meaning. Each color I have chosen brings to mind memories and feelings associated with events that have had a powerful effect on my life. As white light is filtered through the raindrops to create a rainbow, so, too, is God's goodness and holiness filtered through all creation, manifesting itself in each of God's creatures.

God created a universe of color that profoundly affects not only our senses but our emotional, intellectual, and psychological lives. Color even influences our decision-making process. Consider, for example, how we feel when the sky is a gray. Depressed and dreary? Some people cannot live in somber areas and move to where there is more light and color. A light blue sky can brighten our whole day.

Consider also the varied shades of green that burst forth in nature in the springtime in which God has placed us. Think of how it feels walking through a cool, lush, green forest. Compare that with how it would feel to walk through the same forest with all the foliage dark brown or purple. Soft, soothing green certainly does make a difference.

The very way in which God has engineered our physical and emotional makeup renders us dependent upon color. Color enhances the food and drinks we enjoy; black champagne just would not taste the same. A glass of cold brown water does not sound very tempting, even on a hot summer afternoon. We choose our clothes according to color. We paint and design our homes with color being the number-one consideration. We even have books written about our personalities according to color. Millions of dollars are spent each year by market researchers calculating which colors attract consumers and which ones turn them off.

Colors also have metaphorical meanings. White is often used as a symbol of purity, gold as a purifying light, red as passion, purple or violet as a symbol of sin or sorrow for sin, and blue as soothing, comforting, liberating.

As you can see, I think about color a fair amount—and I think about rainbows even more. Rainbows have always been exciting to me, but they became even more significant a few years after my dad's death. Let me tell you the story.

I was off from work on the day that would have been my dad's sixty-eighth birthday, and I decided to visit my mom. It was a three-hour drive to her mom's house. Driving along the lonely highway, I became lost in thought. I became almost hypnotized as I listened to the patter of raindrops on the windshield. Memories of my dad kept flooding my mind, as if he were trying to speak to me. I missed him and wanted to reach out to him. I began talking with my dad and shared with him all that was happening in my life. I wondered if he was pleased with me and proud of what I was doing.

Unfortunately, I started to feel frustrated with this very one-sided conversation. My dad was not responding at all, but I still felt a powerful need to converse with him, not just to talk *to* him. I wanted so much to know how he felt about my life and the work I was doing. I decided to put him on the spot and ask him to give me a sign, to let me know if he was happy with me and proud of my work. I don't know what I expected, maybe a thunderclap, or a voice. But I waited . . . expectantly. It was only minutes later that a brilliant rainbow suddenly appeared in the sky. At first I was thrilled—this was a pretty good sign! But then I started to doubt because, after all, rainbows are really not that uncommon. Why should this one be any different? I decided to up the ante. "Dad, if that is really you, give me a double rainbow!" Almost immediately a second rainbow appeared, just as bright and clear as the first. I started to cry. I knew he was with me.

As I gazed on this scene with wonderment, it occurred to me that the sun is always at the center of the rainbow—no matter what angle or perspective you see it from. The way I looked at it, I saw the sun as God, so I knew my dad was with God and they were being playful together. The two of them were there by my side. I was excited and overjoyed. I felt my dad's embrace as I never felt it before.

I could hardly wait to tell my mom. When I arrived home, I ran into the kitchen and hugged her. Surprised, she asked me, "Dorothy, what happened? Why are you so excited? Are you all right?"

"Mom, the most beautiful thing just happened to me," I told her. As I related the story, she began to cry. We both were quite emotional. "It was so beautiful, Mom. I only wish I had a camera."

That powerful moment became a treasured memory for both of us.

A few days later, after I had arrived back at work in Kalamazoo, I bumped into a parishioner coming into the church. Completely out of the blue he asked in an excited voice, "Dort, did you see that beautiful rainbow the other day?"

"Yes, I sure did. I only wish I could have taken a picture of it."

"Well, guess what, Dort? I did take a picture of it."

"You did? Can I have a copy? I would love to give it to my mom for her birthday next month."

Two weeks later he dropped the photo off at the church.

My next visit home was on my mother's birthday. I presented her with a surprise, the framed picture of the rainbow. I will never forget the surprised look of delight when she opened the package. There were tears and smiles, and she could not speak. It was as if she had seen the face of my dad smiling on her.

Many years later, when she went into a nursing home, she kept that picture by her bedside. Recently my mom passed away, and now she and my dad are celebrating their life together in the presence of Eternal Love.

In the lore of many cultures, the rainbow has been seen as a bridge between heaven and earth, connecting the realm of the spirit with our life in the here and now. This is the way I'd like you to think of the rainbow that is spelled out in this book. The people you'll be meeting in the following pages have bridged the gap between heaven and earth, and have helped bring me closer to God. I share these stories with you in the hope that you also will find in them not just enjoyable reading, but comfort and inspiration.

One

Touched by Red
The Spirit of Love

As a little child, this color became for me a powerful symbol of love, a love that was spontaneous, honest, and genuine, a love that for me needed to be expressed by nothing more than a kind gesture: a red valentine, a red balloon, or even one red rose.

I turned red when I received my first valentine, also red, from someone I admired very much. We were friends in the first grade and are still close friends today.

When I received my first balloon (red, of course), the

excitement I felt was so strong that it still comes back to me when I see a similar balloon today. So I decided to bring such a balloon to friends I visited in the hospital and I was pleasantly surprised by the childlike joy on their faces, when I presented them with a balloon. It touched others the same way it touched me.

In my capacity as campus minister, I made an announcement at all the weekend liturgies about my concern for the sick and lonely in the hospitals and that I was looking for a way to brighten up their lives. I told the students how happy patients were when I brought them a simple colored balloon, and invited them to come to a meeting the following week to discuss a plan of action. Fifty students were interested in the ministry. We set up schedules to visit the hospital on different days, bringing balloons to cancer patients and to children. Though some students had initial doubts about the value of just bringing balloons, they were all pleased that a simple act of giving could bring such joy to the patients.

I was delighted to see how the world blossomed before the students themselves when they saw how easily they could make a real difference in someone's life. I recall one occasion when I was visiting Chris, a friend who was in the hospital. I had brought a student with me, a robust wrestler named Matt. On entering Chris's room, we passed an elderly man in the bed next to him. He looked gaunt and withered from age and loneliness. Immediately on seeing the balloons his eyes sprang to life, thinking they were for him. Nervously, I looked at Matt, then at Chris. Sensing our predicament, Chris looked at me and smiled. "I understand, you can give them to him," he said.

I handed a bright red balloon to Matt. Walking over to the old man's bed, he held out the balloon. The man's face beamed. It was as if he had just been given his first Christmas present. We were all thrilled to see how happy it made the man. With tears in his eyes the old man smiled and said, "Thank you, thank you. This is the first balloon I ever received. I wanted one all my life, but no one ever gave me one."

Matt asked, "How old are you, old-timer?"

"Ninety."

We were shocked. This man had lived all those years without ever receiving a balloon. Tears of joy filled his eyes, and our eyes too.

"It doesn't take much to make people happy," I thought out loud.

We left the hospital that evening with a warm feeling in our hearts. I wondered who benefited more from our visit, the old man or ourselves.

I could tell by the sparkle in his eyes that the red balloon was an expression of love to him.

The following stories show how love is expressed and lived by people I've met along my journey.

Finding Love and Friendship Where I Least Expected

In May 1996 I had the wonderful opportunity of visiting mainland China as part of a group led by Dennis Lou, an adviser to the Chinese government on education and trade matters. At first I was reluctant to go because of all the negative press I had been reading about China, and all the bad news on TV, especially since the Tienanmen Square massacre. Frankly, I was frightened, but I decided to go, after reflecting on one of my favorite Bible verses, "Trust in God with all your heart; do not depend on your own understanding. Seek God's will in all you do, and God will direct your paths" (adapted from Proverbs 3:5–6).

When we arrived in China, we could not have been greeted with more genuine affection and courtesy. As the days passed, we came to realize that the political circumstances of the country could in no way cover up the beautiful spirit of the many people I met. Their kindness and attentiveness, the spontaneity of their friendship, put me at ease and made me feel welcome.

The first place we stayed was an advanced vocational and technical school. The officials and students could not have been more gracious. Their sincere desire to learn all they could about me, about who I was and what I did, made me feel instantly at home. When the students learned that I liked to dance, they pleaded with me to teach them American steps, and arranged to have a dance the following night. Talk about being put on the spot!

Excitement about the presence of visitors and about the dance spread throughout the campus. The next day students and teachers alike approached me to practice their English. Among a thousand different questions, they asked what kind of dances I was going to teach them, where I lived in America, what my family was like, how many brothers and sisters I had. Their excitement was infectious.

When evening came, people began gathering at the dance hall. In no time it was filled. Chinese music was playing softly in the background. The room glowed with soft red lights turned down low. Many of the girls were dressed in red. They were not at all shy about getting out on the dance floor and learning the new steps, thoroughly enjoying the challenge. The boys, just like American boys, were content to sit on the sidelines and girl-watch. It wasn't long, though, before they all caught the spirit, and every boy in the place was dancing. The professors eventually joined in, and even the president of the school took part. The students had never danced with the faculty before, but somehow this night was different. We were just a family of fun-loving young-at-hearts having a good time together. The electric slide seemed to be everybody's favorite. "Now we know some American dances," they cried out happily. The way they danced made obvious their passion for having fun. It brought back memories of my last Easter at Kalamazoo when I had been listening to polka music on my way to church. As I drove into the parking lot and saw the trumpet player waiting for me to open the church, I turned the music up loud and jumped out of the car and said, "Ken, how about celebrating Easter and dancing the polka?" We danced up a storm, laughing so hard that at first we didn't notice my car slowly rolling down the incline toward the street. Fortunately, I caught it just in time. But that didn't stop us from continuing our polka. Totally unaware of anything around us, we didn't notice the pastor driving into the parking lot. Our faces turned red when we realized he was watching. He just shook his head and laughed. "I don't believe you sometimes, Dort."

In the dance hall that night, the Chinese students showed that same childlike joy. Maybe that is why the people I met in China clung to me. They were curious and so many times said to me, "You seem so happy, what is it that brings you such joy? You seem so free, is your family like that too?" They also asked a lot of questions about God. They did not know that I was a nun, which made it all the more surprising. In fact, one afternoon two women interpreters took me shopping. They had been very polite and professional while in business sessions, but now that we were by ourselves and away from their administrators, the ladies in no time at all reverted to being like little girls, laughing and giggling as they encouraged me to try on a bright red kimono. "We love red, even our wedding dresses are red," they told me. The salesladies helping us were delighted to see how much fun we were having. What impressed me the most was the spontaneous warmth and sincerity that flowed from each person I met.

When we visited the University of Shantou, we were given the same warm reception, and became the object of the same curiosity. The people, all so well educated, had the curiosity of little children. Here I was even more impressed with their interest in spirituality. A very bright elderly man who had been the commander of the armies that conquered South China during the revolution expressed a keen interest in spirituality, and said it was something the Chinese people very much needed. This man had also been the mayor of Shantou and built it into the most beautiful and progressive city in the country. He shared his concern about the children's desperate need for role models and spiritual values. The same concern was expressed by Madame Zhu Xi Nan, the director of education for the district of Guilin. The depth of her spirituality came alive after our short encounter.

As I reflect on all my experiences in China, so many thoughts go through my mind: things I saw, things people shared with me, and how these beautiful people touched my life. One for example, still haunts me.

I was horrified by the Chinese government's rigid laws allowing only one child per family. In a conversation one day with a college professor, I asked her bluntly, "Is it really true the government forces you to have abortions?"

"It is the law, but it is enforced only if you are a public official in a prominent position working in Beijing. Otherwise, the government merely fines ordinary citizens for each child after the first one."

She then came back with a remark that startled me. "With all the trouble we have in struggling to keep our children, it is difficult for us to understand why American women are so happy they are allowed to kill their own babies, and we aren't even Christian."

I was too shocked to respond. I wanted to counter what she said, but was lost for words. I've never seen the issue defined so strikingly before. Thinking about it afterward, I became more convinced than ever of the great possibility for spiritual growth that lies in the hearts of the Chinese people.

Although these people have not yet found God, they seem to be yearning for a life that is still beyond their grasp. It broke my heart to feel so helpless in the face of such raw spiritual hunger. I realized I could do nothing to introduce these people to an inner life of the Spirit for which they are starving. It is not rice, fish, or bread the Chinese people crave. It's the spirituality that we in our Western Christian civilization find so easy to lay aside as we bask in material luxury.

My time spent in China made me aware of the needs of my brothers and sisters in faraway places. My experience, so different from all that I read in the papers, has opened my heart to those people, who before were a mystery. Now I know them as people so much like myself, with the same dreams, the same needs, the same struggles to be free from those things that stifle the spirit.

Happily, my relationship with Madame Zhu did not end in China. The following February she was invited by the United States Congress to come to the National Prayer Breakfast in Washington. She was deeply impressed being part of four thousand people praying for one another and for peace in the world. Afterward she came to Joshua to spend time with me. We had a delightful few days. We shared memories of the past and dreams of the future, and stomped through the deep snow like two teenage girls.

When I drove her to the airport to catch her flight home, she said to me, "There are three people who live at Joshua."

"No," I said, "there are only two."

"No," she insisted, "There are three. You, Father Joe, and God. I know, because I felt God's presence there. I know God is there."

I was deeply touched that this gentle, brilliant woman, who did not know of God before, should reveal so much of the richness of her own inner life in so few words.

Her remark brought tears to my eyes. It was such a joy to hear that this gentle, brilliant woman had felt God's presence in our home. It also showed the depth and clarity of her mind that she could reveal so much of herself in so few words.

That this woman, who had previously felt that she did not know God at all should suddenly be shown God's great presence and mercy is amazing to me.

When she left the gate for the plane she could not look back. I am sure she felt the same pain in her heart that I felt in mine. Spirituality comes alive when we know we are loved and accepted for who we are. It was obvious she felt accepted and loved.

People are placed in our life to help us see that God's

goodness is very much alive even where we least expect it. My heart has been touched and colored by the love I received while in China. My experience there was, and continues to be, like a living valentine.

Love—Ever Faithful

When we think of fidelity, we think of it in its ideal form, without blemish, a fidelity that never falters, a fidelity that is like cold steel. Unfortunately, we will never find this ideal in human flesh. Human virtues are the result of lifelong efforts toward an ideal, not the result of instantaneous grace. At the end of life we may have arrived at a certain superior level of faithfulness, but even then we will fall far short of the divine ideal. Human faithfulness should more properly be measured by our tenacity to stay focused on a commitment, whether it be to a person, an ideal, or a cause, no matter how many times we may fall. As humans, we have to expect to fall and stumble along the way. Even Moses, David, and Peter failed God after he placed so much trust in them. What is beautiful in them is their rising up after falling, even falling miserably, and continuing the struggle to be faithful.

It was snowing the day Carrie and Ben were married, but

still the whole town showed up to share their joy. They were a lighthearted, happy couple. Everyone knew they were the perfect match.

For years their marriage was an endless romance. They had so many things in common that it was rare when they were not doing something together. As they were raised in different religious traditions, they decided not to let the Church come between them, so religion was not a part of their life.

As time went on, Carrie grew restless. Something was missing. She still loved Ben immensely and loved being with him, but something was happening at work of which she was totally unaware. Aaron, a fellow employee, started meeting Carrie for lunch, which was quite normal since the employees all went out to lunch together. Gradually, however, subtle changes in Carrie's feelings were taking place. For a while they passed unnoticed. But when she started to find herself getting depressed when Aaron did not show up for lunch, she knew something was happening to her. She was falling in love with him. She panicked. She missed him and felt miserable when they were apart.

At home Ben noticed a change in her but could not understand it. Even though they still enjoyed doing things together, Carrie seemed aloof and irritable, snapping at Ben for the simplest things. When he would ask what was the matter, all she would do was cry. She had always been open and honest with him. Now there was a waterfall of tears that separated them. He felt confused and did not know what to make of this painful change.

Carrie, too, felt miserable. What was happening to her? How could all this have occurred without her realizing what was taking place? How could she ever share with Ben her feelings about Aaron? It would break his heart; he would never understand. For well over a year the relationship deteriorated. The tension between the two became so great, Carrie broke down and finally told Ben everything.

"Are you in love with Aaron?" Ben asked her.

"I think I am" was her embarrassed response.

"How long has this been going on?"

"Well over a year. All we did was go to lunch, in the beginning anyway."

"You mean that all you did was go out to lunch?"

"Well, no, not exactly. It started out like that and, well, I would meet him for dinner the nights I knew you wouldn't be home. I didn't see anything wrong with it. It seemed innocent at first. I enjoyed his company and he was a lot of fun. However, I began to realize that my feelings for Aaron were becoming so strong that I found myself depressed when I could not be with him. It was then that I realized that I had fallen in love, and it was too late."

Ben was devastated. The woman he adored no longer wanted him. He fell apart. He did not know how to cope with such rejection.

Carrie decided to leave home and found a place to live on the other side of town. She needed to understand what was missing in her life, and why it was driving her away from Ben. She knew she still loved him. They even enjoyed making love. Then, what was missing? What more could she want? More affection? More attention? More money? A more exciting romance? Perhaps if she was away from Ben, she could think more clearly.

Aaron satisfied her unfulfilled needs for excitement. He was introducing her to the theater, dancing, horse racing, and exciting new adventures. He took her out to dinner, and sent her flowers for no special reason. This was something her husband had stopped doing years before.

She felt a new happiness. Maybe this was what she was looking for after all. Everything in her life was taking on new meaning. The emptiness seemed to disappear.

Now Carrie had been away from Ben for almost a year, and wondered if she should make the move permanent. She did not want to hurt Ben, but decided it was time to make a decision and get on with her life. While she thought of this difficult choice, she learned that there were other women showing an interest in Ben. This news upset Carrie. The thought of someone else being with Ben was more than she could tolerate. It was then that she began reflecting on her past, and looked at the entire picture. She needed to be sure she was doing the right thing by leaving the man whom she said she still loved but who did not meet all her needs. But does any human being ever fulfill all our needs? Over the years the two seemed to have drifted apart and taken each other for granted. Carrie saw that Ben still meant more to her than she had realized. In many ways Aaron could not hold a candle to him. He was exciting, but was not a man with whom she could share her soul. She could share anything with Ben. Would she be happy without him? If he were not there, could she still be happy?

She decided to go back with Ben. She timidly called him and asked if they could talk. Ben suggested they meet for dinner at her favorite restaurant.

Ben looked haggard and worn and seemed to have aged considerably. He clearly was not taking care of himself. She wore her crimson dress, Ben's favorite. She felt not compassion but a strong sense of guilt over the pain she had caused him.

"Ben, can you possibly forgive me for what I have done?"

"Carrie, I really want to, but it's not easy. I still love you. All I am concerned about is what you need for your happiness. That has always been my concern. In making decisions with you, I never asked myself what I needed, but what was important for your happiness. Even now, with your wanting to come home, I want you to be sure that you will be happy. If not, there is no point of you coming back."

"But didn't you miss me?"

"Of course I missed you, but that is irrelevant to your decision. You can't come back because I missed you. If you come back, it has to be because you want to."

Carrie broke down and cried. "Don't you want me back?"

"Of course I want you back, but I have to get on with my life. I never stopped loving you, but I also have to face reality. I don't think I was doing that for quite some time."

"I am so ashamed of what I did. I don't know if I can deal with all the guilt," she said to Ben.

"That's something I can't do for you. A higher power will have to help you there," Ben said.

They both reached out across the table and kissed. What had begun so painfully became a healing evening.

The next day Carrie gathered her belongings and moved back home with Ben. The move was not easy. She would miss the freedom. She was also anxious about how Aaron would react to her decision. Living away from home had been a hopeful sign to Aaron. Moving back home would upset him.

Aaron did find it difficult to accept her decision. Carrie also struggled. It was painful working so close to him and keeping her commitment to Ben. But her resoluteness made her realize how genuine was her love for Ben. The guilt she felt was good in that it made her aware of her need to change and avoid hurting other people. She was blessed in being able to ask for forgiveness and find peace. Healing is slow and there were many lapses, but her shame made her realize just how much she needed God. We are not bad people. We are just weak and need God's healing and forgiveness. In fact, our weaknesses entitle us to God's mercy. The following words from Scripture are also healing: "My grace is sufficient for you, for power is made perfect in weakness" (2 Cor. 12:9). When we feel we are weakest, it is then that God gives us strength to pick ourselves up and start over, this time with a renewed strength that preserves our self-respect and binds us even more tightly to our commitments. Ben had respect for himself and an understanding love for Carrie that helped him keep his commitment to her.

Now, many years have passed and their love is stronger than ever. Carrie has become more understanding of others in similar situations. It is easy to be judgmental of others when we have not suffered their pain or experienced their weakness.

I tell this story because what happened to Ben and Carrie has happened to many others. Though a spouse may not leave home physically, many leave emotionally with the same effect. This couple had a love for each other that was far beneath the surface. Even though Carrie was preoccupied for a time with superficial unfilled needs, when she realized that these things meant nothing in comparison to her real love for Ben, she came back to him humbled and contrite, and stronger than ever. Ben realized the depth of his own love and knew how much Carrie meant to him. His love was that of a strong man who loved enough to forgive in spite of his pain. There are many lessons in Ben and Carrie's life for married couples, for both husband and wife.

For all of us, fidelity is a never-ending struggle that must be renewed daily as we grow stronger in our commitment. Each day is a new choice, but as we grow, commitment becomes stronger. We may still fall, but our failures will teach us how much we need to look outside ourselves for the strength we do not have within. In that Presence we will find the strength we need.

Ben and Carrie's love is rare. Carrie's heart was like a compass always steering her back to her commitment. Ben's love was like a rock, strong, solid, and unable to be swayed. It is so hard to forgive when our ego is threatened. To see a love so mature, persistent, and forgiving reveals not weakness but a person secure with him or herself. If we love deeply and honestly enough, we will notice and understand the other's pain or unfilled needs. Such a love can be a powerful inspiration to so many today who are hurting and trying to work out their own relationships. The one great difference now in Carrie and Ben's relationship is a spiritual dimension that was missing before. Their relationship, as warm as it may have been, was based only on sharing enjoyable activities. They had been afraid of spiritual bonding. A passage from *The Joy of Full Surrender* by Jean-Pierre de Caussade opened up a new door for them: "We are troubled and disturbed, yet nevertheless in our depths we have some unseen anchor that keeps us clinging to God." Once in that new world of the Spirit, the two grew closer to each other than ever before.

Sometimes a love that has faltered through weakness can emerge stronger than the ostensible love of an unforgiving person who cannot forgive another's weakness. A genuine spirit of love, tested in the ruby-red fires of life's temptations, can grow in ways we never dreamed if we are willing to struggle through those difficult times.

Love Her to Life!

Thirty years ago my Dominican sisters opened a mission in Chimbote, Peru, to work among the poor. My superiors thought it would be a good experience for me to spend a few weeks there, helping the community. I was thrilled because it would give me a chance to see the results of the financial help our campus ministry community—St. Thomas More Student Parish in Kalamazoo—had been providing over the years.

I never realized how difficult was the work our sisters were doing there, and without a salary. Besides working among the poor, they operated a maternity hospital and an outpatient clinic.

The few weeks spent in Chimbote were like nothing I had ever experienced. Life there was so different from ours, simple and unpretentious. The people were poor in material things but much richer in other ways and happier than many wealthy people I knew. The children were enthusiastic and excited about everything, and their joy was contagious. I could see why my Dominican sisters enjoyed working among these remarkable people even though life was so austere. For me it was a privilege to work side by side with these dedicated women. I spent time each day in the hospital helping them with the chores, hoping that I might get a chance to witness a baby being born. When I entered religious life, I thought that would never be a possibility. After only a few days at the mission one of the sisters asked if I would give her a hand. "Yes, I would be glad to. What is it you would like me to do?"

"We are a little short of help today, and wondered if you would like to help us in the delivery room?"

"I would be thrilled. I have always wanted to see the birth of a child."

Seeing the baby being born was like witnessing a miracle. I shook as I held the tiny baby in my hands. What an experience! Tears poured down my cheeks while my heart leapt with joy. At the same time, I felt a tinge of sadness that I would never have a child of my own. As I held the child in my arms, I sensed a mother's happiness and I knew my face was as radiant as a new mother's.

The next day brought another incredible experience. I found myself holding in the palm of one hand a tiny girl who was so small, I wondered how she would survive. From that moment on, I prayed constantly for that helpless little infant.

Every day I visited Dorothea as she was being fed. I loved singing Spanish songs to her while gently rubbing her back as she lay quietly in the incubator. Touch can be healing. Each day Dorothea gained weight. At the end of two weeks she was strong enough to survive. Seeing this child being loved into life was pure joy. I felt God's presence powerfully.

Months after I returned home, I received a letter from the mother of little Dorothea, thanking me for loving her daughter to life. Enclosed was a picture of the two of them. The smile on their faces radiated joy, and they both looked very healthy.

As difficult as the experience had been, I returned home richer and humbler, and with an entirely different view of a simple but authentic spirituality, a faith that went beyond mere attachment to religion. Real spirituality is an ever-deepening understanding of God and of our relationship with God. Although I spent only a short time in Peru, I was strengthened in my own faith and was grateful for all that its people had taught me.

I learned to appreciate not only the love and courage of my sisters working there, but the genuine, sincere warmth and humanness of the simple, poor people who lived there. In spite of their poverty, they were rich beyond anything I experienced. I realized that money does not make one rich, but nobility of soul, which they truly had. Their poverty forced them to live on the edge of despair, but their love and hope expressed itself so touchingly in their sharing with others what little they had. It's strange that the rich rarely have enough to share, while the poor, with their meager belongings, can always find it in their hearts to help those less fortunate. Maybe that is why Jesus loved the poor so much.

Whenever I see the red Peruvian flag now, it brings back all the warm feelings of love I experienced during my stay there.

I Looked into Their Hearts

Driving home from my nephew's baptism, I found myself on a lonely highway, sentimentalizing over the many happy and humorous things that happened and how family can, at times, be such a joy.

Suddenly I heard something in back of the car which at first I thought was a gunshot. When the car began to swerve, I knew one of my tires had blown. Trying hard to control the car, I nudged it off the highway. Although it was only a flat tire, I panicked when I realized I would not get back in time for Mass, where I was expected to direct the music. I had only an hour before I had to be back home. I was never any good at fixing tires, and wearing a white dress was no help. I frantically waved for help at every car that passed. Many people slowed down, looked over out of curiosity, then moved on.

Minutes went by and still no one seemed to care. Finally, an old red pickup truck approached and pulled up in front of my car. Seeing two motorcycles in the back of the truck made me feel uneasy. Two powerfully built young men dressed in black pants and leather jackets emerged from the truck and quietly walked toward me. Realizing I was all alone on this empty highway, a cold feeling of terror came over me. As they approached, I became frightened when I saw the chains around their necks, brass knuckles on their hands, hair hanging down over their shoulders, and their beards in a fairly unkempt state.

But when one of them said in a gentle voice, "How can we help you, ma'am?" it allayed my fear a bit.

"My tire blew out and I need it changed so I can get back to Kalamazoo in time for Mass."

"Piece of cake, ma'am. We'll have you back on the road in no time."

The two men went to work as if they were a pit crew at the Indianapolis 500. They finished in less than ten minutes. I thanked them profusely and offered to give them something. They seemed hurt.

"No way, ma'am. It was a joy. If we can't help a woman in need, what kind of world is it?"

Without another word they walked back to their red truck. As they drove away, I was again struck by how often love is associated with the color red, and that red truck will forever stick in my memory as a reminder of two caring young men.

As I continued on my way home, stunned at what happened, I was embarrassed by my judgmental thoughts. How many times I had judged people by appearances? How wrong I was this time!

I did arrive at the church on time and as I prepared the

readings for Mass, I was again touched by Jesus' words in the Gospel: "You judge by what you see on the surface of people's lives, I judge by what I see in their hearts."

Jesus' message to me was unmistakable. Love sometimes comes to us in the strangest places and from people we least expect.

Divine Spirit of Love,
  Light the flame of love in my heart;
  Seal me with a love
     that sees through your eyes
     that forgives endlessly
     that asks for nothing
     but gives all;
  Surround me with a faithfulness
     that accepts weakness
      without judging
     but believes in commitments;
  Grace me with a love
     that reaches out to all
    no matter
      who they are
      where they came from
      what they have done.
         Amen.

Two

Touched by Orange
The Spirit of Courage

*Whenever I see the color orange I think of the fire in a
blacksmith's forge. The heat made it possible for him to melt the
pig iron and shape it into any form he wanted. Once formed,
it was unbending, strong, and could withstand almost any
kind of abuse. It reminds me of the courage needed and the
strength one must have to stand up for what one believes,
against all odds, even when it means standing alone.
It is relying on God's strength when we encounter
difficulties that are beyond our own resources.*

$\mathcal{I}$t's not easy to stand up for what you believe when those around you continually expect you to conform to their ways. I found that when I am weakest I can find courage in the One who always gives strength to my flagging spirit. The color that symbolizes courage for me is orange. So many coincidences in my life seem to reinforce this feeling.

One day the parent of a child at school gave me an orange monarch butterfly in a shadow-box. Only later did I learn that the butterfly, as fragile as it is, will migrate thousands of miles through difficult weather patterns and life-threatening conditions to reach the place where it will continue its life cycle. No matter what obstacles it encounters, it will not veer off course, but pushes on until it reaches its destination. Every time I see a monarch butterfly, I am reminded of the new life promised to those who have been courageous.

Years ago I watched a blacksmith working at his forge. He kept pumping the bellows to increase the heat of the fire that softened the iron, then beat it with a hammer until it took the shape he wanted. When he finished and the iron cooled, it was hard and firmly set. I never forgot the orange color of the hot metal as it was being pounded into shape. Now that color reminds me of the heat and pressure that toughens our spirit with the courage we need to cope with life's problems and pursue our dreams.

I recall what Robert Kennedy said: "Some men see things as they are and say why. I dream things that never were and say why not." Every now and then we come across people who have that courage to put their dreams into practice. Their stories help us by showing how creative approaches to old problems can make a difference in our lives.

Our spirituality grows from our relationship with God and is often deepened by the difficulties we encounter. If life is too easy, we become complacent with things as they are, and resent strongly the inevitable disturbances of life. When this happens, it is only too easy to close our eyes to the pain and hurt around us. Our spiritual life is basically a love affair with God. When you love someone, you identify with his or her concerns. When Jesus was on earth, his daily concerns were with the poor, the lonely, the brokenhearted. He was sensitive to others' pain. As we grow closer to God, we develop the same sensitivity. True spirituality is measured by our willingness to reach out to those who are hurting and in need.

I remember a sister in our community who followed all the rules and did everything perfectly, but was wrapped up in herself. We shied away from her because she was so critical of the way we did things. If she did something kind for one of us, we resented it because we felt we were merely the object of her charity for that day, and that she really didn't care for any of us. In the same community was another sister, who was a good person with a beautiful heart but was certainly far from perfect. However, when someone needed her she was always there. What is important is our attitude and our motives for the things we do. For Jesus, people were always more important than any rule. Jesus continues to tell us that "the sabbath was made for man and not man for the sabbath." The law was made for God's children and not God's children for the law. Where there is a clash between the law and a real human need, it must be considered whether the law is a good law or is its inflexible application unjust.

The following stories about some very unusual people show how helping others added a remarkable dimension to their lives.

Courage to Follow a Dream

A latecomer to my world is a man who on the surface seemed so ordinary. Once I got to know him, I found a sensitive and adventurous spirit, a person willing to take risks. Risks are never easy. For a prominent person, failure can be devastating.

Bill ran the family company, Matthew G. Norton Heavy

Equipment Co., in Seattle, Washington. He was also on the boards of Alaska Airlines and the Weyerhaeuser Lumber Company.

Even though he was a successful businessman, something was missing. He felt a need to do something that would make a difference in people's lives.

At that time the International Children's Games were being held simultaneously in a number of countries. When these Goodwill Games came to Seattle, Bill found his chance to become involved. He volunteered to produce the closing ceremony. It meant endless meetings with organizers, city officials, Games planners, police, and entertainers as well as community fund-raisers. Given free rein to shape the closing ceremony, he decided to focus the pageant around children's role in peace. Admission was free and youth groups were recruited. The theme song chosen for the ceremony went "If we all lit just one little candle, what a bright world this would be." Its finale included a live satellite television hookup with children gathered at Red Square in Moscow and at Westlake Mall in Seattle, singing the same song and waving glow sticks, representing little candles, in the darkness. He told me his inspiration for this was the book *Joshua and the Children*.

The ceremony was deeply moving, not only for those who attended and took part, but for the millions throughout the world who watched it on television.

Bill sensed that the ceremony was not just the closing of an event but the beginning of something new and beautiful in his life.

During the production of the event he was contacted by a man named Sam, the executive director of an international grass-roots advocacy organization that had remarkable success in "creating the will to end poverty" by promoting successful models. One such model was micro-enterprise lending, also known as "village banking." Bill and his wife were invited to view these programs in El Salvador. The experience made a profound impression. The micro-banks are really collectives of twenty-five to thirty poor women who meet in their homes and use small loans as capital to fuel fledgling businesses such as rolling tortillas, selling clothes, raising chickens, and making blouses. It is amazing to see how much can be done with less than a hundred dollars, and what a dramatic impact starting a small business can have on the quality of life for someone living at poverty level. I was pleasantly surprised to discover that the repayment rate of these small loans was over ninety-seven percent—much better than for most banks! Over the next year Bill traveled to other third world countries and saw further examples of the enormous hope these micro-enterprise lending programs gave to millions of people. He saw the potential for creating loan programs with help from the private sector that could be cost-efficient. This could even permit borrowers to eventually compete for credit just like other businesses.

Bill and his wife, Paula, began Global Partnerships in 1994 with the help of many dedicated people and launched a model micro-enterprise program in Guatemala. Today they have four thousand borrowers and twenty thousand family members, and the list is still growing. Their dream is to grow sixfold in the next three years.

The couple initiated this program in Guatemala because of the dire poverty in that country and the lack of access to capital. Bill said that the Guatemalans have become not just business clients but neighbors and good friends. The work Bill and Paula are doing there will affect the lives of generations to come. What the couple has learned in Guatemala they are now applying here at home and in other places. They have come to realize that the world has grown so small that we can no longer consider anyone a stranger, no matter how far away he or she may live, and that even the smallest gestures of goodness can have global implications.

A critical factor in Bill's decision to become involved in micro-credit was his realization that business people in high places have a lot of goodwill and a wealth of experience. They have an abundance of knowledge, talents, and resources, and would like to help others but do not know where to start. Bill decided to tap this important reservoir. He was overwhelmed at how many were willing to help.

These people, who had never been involved in projects like this one, helped the poorest of the poor fulfill dreams they had never thought possible, and gave hope to those living each day on the edge of despair. It was a thrilling experience for all who worked on the project.

Many people ask Bill, "Why do you do this?" "What's in it for you?"

Bill's answer was simple.

"When I know that every day thirty-five thousand children die needlessly of easily preventable diseases, when I see millions permanently crippled by polio, blinded by vitamin deficiency, or permanently disabled by malnutrition, I can't sit back and do nothing. There are no limitations to what today's technology can achieve. The only limitation is the lack of will to do something. We can make a difference if only we are willing to reach out and help our brothers and sisters in need."

We all can make a difference, but sometimes prejudice and apathy inhibit us from reaching out to others. We are all gifted and talented in many ways. There is something each of us can do to make this world a better place, but we have to be willing to take the risk.

Bill placed himself in circumstances that demanded more than just one risk. What he did took not only generosity, but courage. It is rare to come across a person of his stature and social position who is willing to step out in the troubled world and try to make a difference. Bill's example made me think about the times in my own life when I reluctantly took risks and saw them pay off in ways I could never have anticipated. When I was invited to do campus ministry, my only prior experience was working with junior high students, certainly no preparation for working at a college. Even one of the interviewers told me I didn't have the background to work at that level. But that didn't discourage me, I was confident that it was where I was being led. I always loved working with young people. To me, college students still had very much of the child in them. I will forever be grateful to the pastor who headed the campus ministry team for insisting that I take the job. Now, when I look back and see the thousands of young college students who came back to their faith because of our team efforts, I thank God for giving me the courage to take that risk.

Of course, Bill's venture was on a much grander scale than mine. It must have taken a great deal of courage for him to embark on a project with so many possibilities for failure. But his vision and courage were well rewarded.

Seeing people's lives change from destitution and despair to success in the business world fills the heart with joy. "Come, blessed ones! When I was desperate and without hope, you taught me how to dream again and showed me how to fulfill that dream." Just like the orange fire in the blacksmith's forge that melted iron, Bill's love was the fire that helped mold the lives of the poor into what they had been dreaming of for so long, a chance to be successful and independent. There are so many people who hunger for the opportunity to make something of themselves if given a chance. Bill gives these people a chance to fulfill their dreams. If we can take the time to see our sisters and brothers who are searching for a place in this world and give them an opportunity not only to make a difference, but to share their gifts, then the fire of our own love can also melt their frozen hearts, which have been hurt by life's pain and injustice.

Watching the Children Dream Their Dreams

Jesus said, "Behold, I make all things new." This was the quote Archbishop Maida of Detroit used when he shared his vision of the city before the Economic Club of Detroit.

In his talk the archbishop expressed his deep concerns about the community. He offered to club members a plan he felt could bring new hope to thousands of young people whose future seemed bleak, if not hopeless. The plan envisioned a partnership between industry, business, and education. People of all denominations would work together initiating educational programs. The heart of this dream was a system of ecumenical schools, where children of all denominations could learn together in a healthy, disciplined environment where spiritual values reigned.

The archbishop's talk sparked a response rare among businessmen. Word circulated and enthusiasm spread. The plan was so simple yet so practical, so utterly attainable. With the archbishop's continued guidance and influence, everyone felt the project could become a reality. In a short time the ideas and proposals took shape. The whole concept had to be based on a strong foundation of faith as well as a determined pursuit of academic excellence. And the school had to be open to all children of the city, regardless of social or economic status.

When it came to tuition, it could not go beyond the means of the parents. Since the cost for educating a child in this system would be approximately $4200 a year, it was decided to set the tuition at $1850. The balance would be covered by voluntary contributions. No child would be turned away because of inability to pay. But it was not to be free. Parents or whoever was responsible for the child would have to make a commitment to the child's education and be involved in the process.

The school would operate within the framework of a partnership program. The partner, who would sponsor a child, would come to the school three or four times a year for an hour and show personal interest in the student's project. Each partner would commit him or herself to two thousand dollars per child. Sometimes it was an individual, sometimes a corporation or foundation.

Cornerstone is a system of Christ-centered ecumenical schools. Its goal is to build in children a strong faith as well as a desire for academic excellence. For the program to work, it needed the support of the students' families to extend the development of moral and spiritual values, and sense of responsibility to the community, and into the nonacademic arena.

The leaders aimed to foster healthier family environment and a personal satisfaction in learning. This would result in a much higher percentage of graduates and would demonstrate the school's value.

When the first school opened, those concerned were apprehensive, but their fears turned out to be unfounded. The community responded enthusiastically, as people's involvement testified. Others asked if they could join the committee, a suburban bank president and two inner-city ministers in particular. Before long it was clear the venture would be a success. At that point the archbishop knew his help would no longer be needed, so he stepped aside and let others run the entire operation.

The admission policy for the school as well as the curriculum were modeled after the Gospel message: "Let the little children come to me." Every child is precious to God.

Children need to be prepared for challenging times ahead, for themselves and for the country. Touching a child's mind and soul can inspire that child to become what God dreamed. All a child needs is to be given a chance. These children, some middle-class, some poor, some with no parents, or only one parent, many disadvantaged in some way, are given the chance to make something of themselves.

A school year consists of 240 days of instruction as compared to the traditional 180. The curriculum offers the basics in reading, writing, and arithmetic, the A-Beka phonics curriculum, and art and music programs.

The school is Christ-centered and seeks to develop the whole child through Bible study, daily encouragement, positive behavior reinforcement, chapel, prayer, song, and positive role models.

Although the program has been in operation for only a short time, the change that has taken place in many of these children is remarkable.

Newspapers, magazines, and other media, have reported on this wonderful educational venture. It has been successful. Presently, in two elementary schools and one middle school, over four hundred children are enrolled with over three hundred on the waiting or inquiry list. Seeing the various churches working together is in itself an inspiration. Classes are held in the former Sacred Heart Seminary, and in the former Lutheran School for the Deaf. When people see the positive effects this program has not only on the children but on the family and the community as well, interest spreads.

People from as far away as California, Texas, and New York have asked to be partners. Two of the three Detroit auto makers are supporting the program.

I cannot express my delight over the simplicity and success of this program. I am always thrilled to see the dramatic change in children when a teacher takes a personal interest. To me it means the successful fulfillment of a school's mission: to inspire children. To witness this in a new school system is thrilling. I am certain Cornerstone will grow and spread far beyond Detroit. God bless the caring bishop and concerned business people who had the courage to embark on such a new and untried venture. I only wish I could have worked with them. It would be a happy continuation of the work I did for so many years.

Teachers have the privilege of preparing students to be the person of their dreams. I treasure my years as a teacher and am grateful for the opportunity to have shared with children healthy values and beliefs. Watching them develop into beautiful adults over the years is a joy like no other.

I admire the archbishop for having the courage to dream what might have seemed to others impossible. To dream a dream and share it with no one else is good fantasy, but to share a dream that may seem impossible to some takes rare courage. To offer to stand by a dreamer's side and work with him as he takes his first steps in a revolutionary project is not easy. Those who have had the courage to initiate such ventures must surely have gone through many difficult times, but, hopefully, emerge as steadfast as the blacksmith's forged steel.

Courage Made This Dream Come True

Over the years the federal and local governments have been pumping hundreds of millions of dollars into massive housing projects, which they now admit have been a failure. Not only did they not solve the problem of housing poor people, they crammed people into already crowded high-rises far from any possible place of employment or recreation. As I travel from city to city on speaking engagements, I see more and more of these abandoned ghost towns in the heart of our cities.

Occasionally, a businessman with a heart and a dream will conceive a plan that is not just another fantasy, but a practical, workable vision with the potential for solving not just the housing problem, but the many other problems related to poverty. Here are the stories of two of these vision-aries, not only people with a heart, but with the common sense and genius for organizing and executing their dreams.

John, a community activist in Detroit, has been working in the inner city for the past eight years on a project that he and some friends initiated.

He called it the Joshua Project. They have invited Habitat for Humanity to work with them as partners in one phase of their project. Since they started, they have already built seventeen new homes in Westwood Park, renovated twenty-four others, and created a neighborhood preservation plan with residents of that area. They also demolished fifty-six dangerous structures throughout the city of Detroit and worked with police to eliminate gang activity and drug sales in Westwood Park. They are working with postal officials in planning a new post office for the Brightmoor area.

Hundreds of volunteers from the neighborhood have been working together on these projects and are so proud of the beautiful homes they built. However, these dedicated people are not in the business of building just homes, but of gathering together people in the neighborhood to inject new life into every facet of these horribly blighted areas.

Rebuilding community is their motto; it is instilling pride and a sense of self-worth in the people involved. Residents of a community who renovate their neighbor's home now have a sense of pride. Things are different; practically everyone is working, and the streets and play areas are clean. As the inhabitants of a neighborhood look around and see the fruits of their hard work, they cannot but feel a sense of dignity and pride. What they accomplished is as pretty as a butterfly freed from its cocoon. I remember taking a group of college students to work in Appalachia for a week, and the good feeling we had after helping people repair homes and clean up yards. We made it fun and didn't mind the hard work. The happy look on people's faces was reward enough. We laughed as we discussed all that we had been doing, things we would have never have dreamed of doing back home, like putting up walls, wallpapering, repairing roofs, and installing septic systems.

Whenever we are courageous enough to accept challenges, we develop gifts and talents we may not have been aware of that have been hidden for years. It is amazing how willing God is to share the divine ability to create and make all things new.

The Power of Golf

In Atlanta, another vision is taking shape, the rebirth of an old, run-down neighborhood, this one in a remarkable setting, next to one of the oldest and most renowned golf courses in the country. A contractor named Tom, with a vision and a heart, saw a way of using the enormous economic power of golf to revitalize an urban community in distress.

The East Lake community includes the historic East Lake Golf Club, home course of golf legend Bobby Jones and one of the great golf courses of the world. This course was once a vital part of Atlanta, but steadily deteriorated in the 1960s.

The golf club mirrored the adjacent East Lake Meadow housing project, dilapidated and abandoned. People avoided both places.

In 1994 Tom purchased the club and donated it to his family's foundation. He charged the foundation with the singular task of restoring the golf course as a memorial to Bobby Jones, and used it as a catalyst to spark the revitalization of the whole surrounding neighborhood.

Through a twenty-five-million-dollar purchase and renovation effort, Tom's foundation has brought the course and clubhouse back to its original condition. The East Lake Golf Club is transforming the neighborhood. Surplus income donated to the East Lake Community Foundation supports long-term educational, spiritual, and recreational programs; it encourages socially responsible corporations as members of the club to donate at least two hundred thousand dollars to the foundation. This money in turn enables the golf club to create jobs for the community, especially for young people. This then attracts commercial and retail investments in the neighborhood.

The restoration of the club has already created 193 new jobs, and its caddie program offers more than one hundred high-paying jobs for students after school, as well as during the summer.

The public course is expected to attract at least seventy thousand new visitors each year to the neighborhood, and to create demand for even more retail business investments.

Through a joint venture the Atlanta Housing Authority and the East Lake Community Foundation will tear down and replace the old buildings with five hundred affordable housing units on a seventy-five-hundred-acre site. This phase will accommodate a mixed-income community. The development will include an eighteen-hole public golf course, tennis courts, public parks, an elementary school, and a YMCA.

A golf academy, as part of the club's program, will be a component of the recreational training available. Acceptance into the program will be contingent on faithfulness to homework and school assignments. Golf professionals will be available for the golf lessons. The same rules apply for the tennis academy. A new fifty-thousand-square-foot

YM/YWCA will be constructed to offer a wide range of programs, including art, music, dance, and a radio station run by young people.

By 1996 approximately 140 children entered kindergarten at Drew Elementary and East Lake Elementary, the two public schools included within East Lake. As it relates to education, the goal of the East Lake Community Foundation is simple: to insure that by the year 2009 every one of the school's students presently attending will graduate from high school and enter college or other post–high school education program.

This educational initiative, a joint effort of the foundation, Georgia State University, and the Atlanta Public Schools, will carry out this mission in phases.

Phase One will concentrate on after-school programs involving the golf and tennis academies and the YMCA, devised by Georgia State University experts.

In Phase Two the foundation will sponsor a preschool developed and run by Georgia State University and designed to provide neighborhood children with a solid foundation in early childhood skills.

Phase Three will focus on programs and reforms within the public schools themselves. The goal is to decentralize the schools, increase parental and community involvement, and provide specialized training for teachers.

Tom had the courage to connect people of different income levels and diverse backgrounds, revive a dying community, and give its children reason to strive for dreams that before would have been unthinkable. Like the village blacksmith, whose forge could fashion out of nothing something beautiful, Tom's courage is transforming a whole neighborhood.

Divine Spirit of Courage,
Give me courage
to face my fears;
confidence
in taking risks.
Make me patient and wise in
opposing injustice;
calm and steadfast
when faced with rejection;
honest and trustworthy
when confronted with deceit;
peaceful
when surrounded by turmoil;
silent
in the face of criticism.

Amen.

Three

Touched by Yellow

The Spirit of Joy

*When I think of yellow it often reminds me of the
yellow brick road in The Wizard of Oz that led Dorothy
to her rainbow of joy.
The lightness of yellow brings to mind joy
and enthusiasm for living.*

I remember as a child walking along the road near my
home and looking at the fields covered with yellow-
eyed daisies swaying in the breeze as if waving to me as I

walked past. I would clap my hands and jump up and down with delight. It made me so happy.

Ever since, I have always loved these flowers and a bouquet of daisies still brightens my day.

I guess I have always been a happy person. Maybe joy comes more easily to me than to many others. While there is a certain amount of personal choice in whether we are happy or sad, I think each of us has an underlying spirit that drives our lives. My underlying spirit seems to be joy. Even when I was a child my dad would say, "Dort, we love to see you smile. You make us happy even when we feel down."

A guitar strap given to me years ago has smiling faces on it and serves as a constant reminder to be happy. A colorful sign, BLESSED ARE THE SMILE MAKERS, has hung on my office door for years, reminding me to help others to be happy. To this day the smiling face has been my signature for those who know me. It isn't that my life has always been full of sunshine, but I try not to let dark clouds overshadow my personality.

When I meet people excited about life, their happiness is infectious and I cannot help but feel God's presence. It reminds me of words I once read on a card, "When you see people filled with enthusiasm, you know they have a joy that comes from God."

God has given each of us free will. How we choose to

exercise it will determine how peaceful and joyful we will be. Joy comes from inner peace—peace with God and peace with ourselves. To walk in the light of God is to walk in peace and joy. God sent us light so we don't have to stumble in the dark.

Buried Alive

At some Thanksgiving celebrations we may have a hard time finding things to be thankful for, at others we thank God for giving us joyful experiences we will never forget.

Father Jim, a friend of mine who works in Alaska, told me this powerful story about a family in his neighborhood who experienced a frightening incident just before Thanksgiving. Their names were Debbie and Dougal.

The day before Thanksgiving, Dougal was returning home by snowmobile from a neighboring village and called his wife to tell her he was on his way. The trip started out as a routine run across the meadow that led home, but at some point he wandered dangerously from the trail without realizing it and wound up driving across the partly frozen snow-covered river. Too late he saw a huge hole in the ice in front of him. Dougal and the snowmobile plunged through the ice into the freezing, fast-flowing river. Struggling to the edge of the hole, he managed to grab the ice before the current sucked him under. Holding on with all his strength, he struggled for almost an hour until he finally pulled himself out of the water.

Exhausted, his heavy clothes and boots soaked, he lay motionless in the snow. The air temperature was below zero and his clothes began to freeze. Out in the middle of nowhere, he knew his only hope was to keep moving. He picked himself up and started walking, but each step became more painful. The ice was penetrating his clothes and reaching his flesh. He walked for almost half a mile before collapsing, but continued to drag himself another hundred feet, until he ran out of strength. The heavily falling snow quickly covered his body.

Unable to call for help or to let anyone know his whereabouts, he lay in the snow, terrified by his helplessness and the realization that he would probably freeze to death. "How long before someone will find me, if ever? Will I die out here? Will I freeze to death? I can't move anymore. Dear God, help me!"

Alerted by his earlier phone call, his wife knew when she should expect him. When he failed to show up, she began to worry, since the snow was falling so heavily. She called her friends and neighbors asking what should be done. They immediately gathered and formed a search party.

They followed the trail they all knew well. On their way they encountered two other neighbors, Louis and Clinton, who offered to help but thought it best to take an alternate route. After searching for almost six hours, one of the snowmobiles hit a bump, which jolted it. Seeing a boot protruding from the snow, the two men jumped off their vehicles and brushed away the snow. It was the body of their friend. They noticed the snowmobile had struck his head. Quickly pulling his unconscious body out of the snow, they tried to revive him. Dougal was frozen stiff. There were hardly any signs of life as they rushed him back to Koyukuk, fifteen miles away, immediately brought him to the town clinic, and called the hospital in Fairbanks for instructions, since there were no doctors on duty. The doctor they reached told them step by step what they should do to start the thawing process, while waiting for the airplane to arrive and transport Dougal to Fairbanks, an hour and a half away. After spending seventeen days in Fairbanks, he was flown to Anchorage for rehabilitation. At the end of his recovery, which was almost total, Dougal had suffered a partial loss of memory and lost the fingers on both hands.

It is obvious that there wasn't just one miracle that happened that night, but a string of them. During the summer months, very few have ever endured the ice-cold river for more than twenty minutes and lived. It is almost unheard of that anyone survived the river in wintertime.

Father Jim asked Dougal how he felt about losing all his fingers. He responded, "I'm just glad to be alive."

"He has never displayed any anger or bitter feeling about anything, only gratitude," said Debbie.

Never did the family have more reason to be joyful and grateful than they did on that Thanksgiving day.

A thousand things happen to each of us every day for which we have many reasons to be grateful. We do not have to wait for some dramatic event, nor do we have to wait until Thanksgiving to say thanks to God. And when it comes to loved ones, we never appreciate them more than when we face the danger of losing them. The golden sun never shined brighter than on the day Debbie and Dougal were reunited after his recovery.

You Can Do It. I Believe in You!

It was a beautiful, crisp winter day. The sun was bright and fresh snow covered the ground like a blanket. Joy filled the air.

I was having music practice with the children at St.

Tom's in Kalamazoo in preparation for our Christmas liturgy. Children were volunteering for solo verses they wanted to sing, and one little boy raised his hand.

"Sister Dorothy, can I please sing the alleluia verse this year for Jesus' birthday?"

"Sure, Glen, that would be such a nice gift. We will have to practice it over and over, you know."

"That's okay. I really want to do it. I promise I will do my best."

"Glen, if you get nervous, just try this: Inhale Jesus, exhale anxiety. You will be surprised how it will help you to relax."

Glen had been adopted by Ray and Carlene when he was two and a half years old. His biological mother was a hundred-dollar-a-day heroin addict. Both were badly abused physically and emotionally, but were still enthusiastic about life. Glen wanted so much for his adoptive parents and family to be proud of him, so he asked if I would practice with him.

On Christmas Eve the children were gathering for a final warmup and were dancing around like sugar-plum fairies. Glen beamed. He was so proud and happy. He had practiced his verse for days, and now one final time before Mass. He sang it perfectly. I gave him a hug to reassure him.

Joy radiated from their faces as the children processed

into church singing. When the time came for Glen's big moment, he stood up with all the confidence in the world. I was so proud of him. He began singing the verse like an angel, but halfway through it, seeing himself all alone in front of the assembly, he panicked and slid off key, never to return. He looked so disappointed. As our eyes met, I smiled to assure him that it was okay.

After Mass he ran up to me and said, "I know you are not mad, but I am so sorry I messed it up."

I reached out and hugged Glen, saying, "That's okay, Jesus understands even if no one else does. He knows it came from your heart. That's all that matters. Don't let this discourage you, Glen; you can do anything if you set your heart on it."

"Thanks for believing in me," he said as he left.

Seven years later, Glen surprised me after Mass one Sunday morning. He came over and said, "Sit down, I have a gift for you."

I did not know what to expect. He began singing "God Bless America." His rich, trained baritone voice echoed throughout the church. It was beautiful. I was extremely touched. When he finished, I ran over and hugged him.

He said, "This is my thank-you for believing in me." We hugged again with tears in our eyes.

Carlene and Ray loved him and wanted the best for him.

They had sent him to Boys Town in Omaha, Nebraska, where he graduated and received a certificate as a nurse's aide. He worked at a nursing home and then did home care.

Glen succeeded at Boys Town. He became a soloist in the Boys Town choir, "Voices." His big debut came when he was asked to sing "Sweet Little Jesus Boy" at the Boys Town Christmas banquet for over two thousand employees.

He later told me: "I was so afraid I would mess it up, but I remembered you telling me to inhale Jesus and exhale anxiety. I did it! Then I said a little prayer to Jesus and did my best. I was surprised how easily it went.

"The highlight of my life was when I was asked to sing the national anthem at the College Baseball World Series held in Omaha. I felt I was in heaven. I didn't want to mess this one up, so I said my little prayer and it went great!"

At Boys Town five students are hand-picked to conduct tours through the facility, and Glen was proud to be one of the five chosen. One day, a stockbroker connected with a well-known investment firm was in one of Glen's tour groups. He was so impressed with Glen's presentation and excellent manners that he went to the director of Boys Town and asked if Glen could come and work for him after graduation. He also promised that his firm would cover expenses for his college education. The broker thought Glen would be an excellent public relations officer. Glen is now a full-time college student majoring in public relations with a minor in music. When he has time, he works for the company, entertaining clients, sometimes traveling to other cities, meeting with potential clients.

Glen said to me recently, "Sister Dorothy, as I was growing up, things were very difficult and the future looked bleak. During that difficult time, you were the 'wind beneath my wings.' You gave me the courage and confidence I needed. I am involved in music now because you helped me to love it. Thanks so much."

What I did was very little, but then, it does not take much to affirm someone. Children need encouragement; they are frightened by life. They need to understand they have gifts and that it is important for them to develop and use these gifts. Many children's gifts lay dormant because no one has taught them to recognize and nurture those gifts. It makes a difference when someone believes in you and encourages you to use your gifts. Sometimes it takes only a word or a smile.

Glen is only one example of what can happen when someone cares. He is clearly a changed person. He is happy and confident, radiating joy wherever he goes, because someone believed in him, saw his goodness and brought out the best in him. When we develop the abilities given us by God, our whole being comes to life and reflects the joy we feel within.

Glen was shown his golden road and had the courage to follow where it led, to the wonderful land of dreams and opportunities that has made possible for him to touch the hearts of many with his beautiful, confident singing voice.

*H*ow can one talk about joy without talking about children? Their innocence and freshness is like a field of daisies. They still have that sense of wonder that so many of us have lost along the way. They are still awed with the thrill of Christmas and Santa Claus bringing them presents. They are fascinated with everything they hear about the mysterious God their parents talk about. They are almost like little theologians with their endless questions about God and that unseen world where God lives. The following stories express some of that childlike wonder.

God Is Still Alive!

Children can ask the most amazing questions. While I was visiting my sister, her four-year-old daughter, Colleen, asked her, "Mom, is God dead?"

Shocked that she would ask such a question, she said, "Colleen, whatever possessed you to think such a thing?"

" 'Cause you said that Grandpa's dead and he's in heaven with God. God must be dead too."

Still surprised at her daughter's strange logic, she said, "Why don't you ask your aunt Dort. She's good with those kind of things; she'll tell you."

Colleen came running into the family room and cuddled up next to me on the sofa. "Aunt Dort, Mom said that Grandpa is with God and Grandpa is dead, so is God dead?"

"God's home is in heaven, Colleen. God does not have to die to get there. God lives there, but we have to die to be with God."

"So God's still alive, then?"

"Yes, very much alive."

"Okay, I feel better now. I don't know what I'd do if God died."

"I don't either, Colleen. But you'll never have to worry about that, because God can't die. He's eternal.

"It means God always was alive and always will be alive."

That seemed to make her happy, so she jumped off the sofa and skipped out to tell her mother the good news.

Life is new to children. They are always trying to figure it out. They view everything with such a sense of wonder. I think this is why Jesus loved little children so much. He was thrilled with the simple joy they found in life and the trust they placed in others. We can help them by answering them with the same simple candor with which they pose their questions.

A Child's Insight

Sunday morning after Mass, a mother brought her son to show me that he knew how to bless himself before prayers.

"Jonathan, show Dorothy how you bless yourself before prayers."

He proudly began, "In the name of the Father, the *Mother*, the Son, and the Holy Spirit. Amen."

"Jonathan, that is not how I taught you."

He looked up at his mother with his hands on his hips and said, "Mom, everyone knows that if there is a Father and Son, there has got to be a Mother."

She smiled and shook her head.

"Well, you certainly have an intelligent son," I said to her. "Be careful, he may be a theologian someday."

Children view things with such simple logic. The obvious, which so often escapes us, they pick up immediately. They challenge us to rethink the simple things in life that we frequently overlook. Jesus said, "Let the children come to me and do not hinder them, for of such is the kingdom of heaven," which was his way of promising that if we could be honest, trusting, loving, and forgiving like a child, we need not fear losing heaven. The innocence of a child is so refreshing. They have not learned to be deceitful or hateful. They speak from the simplicity of their hearts.

Wisdom, like a bright golden light, bursts forth at a tender age and springs upon us unawares. As a simple flower can brighten a gloomy day, so a child's simple question can catch us by surprise and reawaken our own sense of wonder.

Nothing Is Impossible

Once while visiting my mom at the nursing home, I wheeled her to chapel for prayer. Outside the chapel a priest was talking to a little boy. I heard him ask the boy what he would like Jesus to send him for Christmas.

The boy spelled out the list, and at the end said, "But what I really want most of all is to be possible."

"Be possible? What do you mean, you want to 'be possible'?" the priest asked, confused by such a strange request.

"My parents keep telling me, 'You're impossible, you're

impossible.' I guess I make them unhappy, so I asked Jesus to make me possible so my parents can be happy this Christmas."

"You're not a bad boy, are you?" the priest asked.

"I don't think so, but I think I confuse my parents sometimes, and they don't know what to do with me. So they say I'm impossible. And I don't want to be impossible."

"I think you mean you would like to do things so your parents could understand you better."

"I guess so."

"Well, don't you worry, son, we are all impossible sometimes because God made each of us different. Just because others have a difficult time understanding us doesn't mean we're bad. It just means we are different. And it is okay to be different as long as we are doing good. I am sure your parents love you even if they can't understand you sometimes, so don't you worry about that anymore. On Christmas, just tell your parents you love them and they'll be happy. I am sure they would not want you to be any different from what you are."

Thinking for a moment, the boy looked up at the priest and said, "I feel better now, because I didn't know how I could be any different than I am. I hope Jesus gives you what you want for Christmas, Father."

"Thank you, son."

When we are young, we so often are told that things are impossible. When I was a child, anything like a computer would have seemed impossible. If someone said, "Too bad we have to walk up stairs. Why can't they move?" that would have sounded ridiculous. We may have talked about the man in the moon, but no one ever dreamed of a human ever landing there. As we live, we learn that some of the "impossibles" of our childhood are now realities. For example, we take moving walkways from one airline to another, pick up an electronic ticket, and get on a plane that takes us to countries thousands of miles away in a matter of hours. We take our cellular phones and carry on conversations with friends hundreds of miles away as clearly as if they were in the same room. We watch wars on television as the battles are taking place. We have computers that can communicate with people halfway around the world in seconds. And, what seemed most impossible of all, people did land on the moon. What would have been an impossibility a few decades ago is now commonplace. How stunning are these endless creations of the "impossible."

We ourselves are also "possible" and joyful when we are using the gifts and talents with which God has blessed us. I never thought I would be traveling around the world giving talks or writing a book. But after all these years I find myself doing just that. It is amazing the seemingly impossible things we find ourselves doing when we open our hearts and let God guide us along that "impossible" way.

"God Comes to Visit You Instead"

A group of young boys approached their parish priest. "Father, do you have a few minutes?"

"Yes, why?"

"Come with us, we want to show you something."

"Where are we going?"

"Just wait and you'll see."

After walking six or eight blocks, they stopped at a two-story house and rang the bell. They entered, then walked up the stairs to the second floor.

A woman in her late thirties opened the door and let them in. "Hello, boys, are you here again? Oh, I didn't see you, Father. Come right in."

As they entered the dining room, they saw a teenage boy sitting at the table. He was in a wheelchair. On the table in front of him was a miniature band saw. With his two hands the boy was guiding very thin pieces of wood along a stenciled pattern. At one point his right hand slipped and fell to his side. His mother walked over, lifted his arm, and placed his hand back on the table. It was clear he had no control over his arms. He was quadriplegic.

When the boy saw his friends enter, his face lit up. "I'm so glad you came. I was just sitting here, putting some things together."

The boy sat back in his wheelchair and relaxed as his friends sat around the table with him. They introduced the priest to their friend. The boy joked that he had heard a lot about his parish priest but never had a chance to meet him, since he never went to church. "You don't have to worry about that, son," the priest told him. "God comes to visit you instead. You're lucky."

"You're right. I am, Father, in more ways than one. I always feel so happy. It must be a special gift from God. Some people don't think so, and think I'm missing out because I am not like others. Even my mother feels sorry for me. They can't seem to understand that I am perfectly happy the way I am, and I look forward to each day."

At that point one of the boys said, "Father, you should see all the things he makes. Tony, show the priest all your unique creations."

Tony's mother wheeled him into the living room, where there were shelves full of ornately carved and decorated objects. Music boxes, replicas of famous buildings, jewel boxes, and a dozen other objects. The largest one was a chandelier with countless tiny lights. Tony's mother looked so proud, and commented, "My son was offered ten thousand dollars for that chandelier, and he refused to sell it." Everyone stood around admiring his beautiful works of art as his mother wheeled him back to the table.

"Tony, show the priest how you carve the wood."

A little embarrassed, Tony began to slide the wood through the saw slowly, painstakingly. It was all done with unbelievable patience and precision. Yet you could see a look of peace on the boy's face.

Staying for a few minutes longer, the boys finished off the soda Tony's mother had offered them. A short time later they left.

Walking down the street, the boys said, "Well, Father, what did you think? Isn't it a joy to see something so beautiful?"

"It really is. It is a living sermon."

While Tony's story is a powerful one, I have come across so many people with problems who face life with an incredible sense of adventure. Another young man I met had the same problem as Tony. He did not let his disabilities interfere with his zest for living. He drove three thousand miles to attend a university in California, where he earned his degree in education, and later celebrated his graduation with a trip to the Grand Canyon and a white-water rafting adventure down the Columbia River. He then drove cross-country to visit his parents. He has since married and now teaches children with learning disabilities.

His joyful spirit touches the hearts of everyone who meets him.

I will never forget a talk given by a bishop with a severe physical handicap. After joking about his own handicap, he talked about how all of us are handicapped in one way or another. His handicap was visible. Many of ours are known only to ourselves. Some we may not even be aware of. Each of us has limitations, some of which are severe.

Einstein was handicapped. He flunked mathematics in school. He had a severe learning problem. Winston Churchill was manic-depressive. Every one of us has some sort of moral, mental, or physical handicap. We struggle for a lifetime to overcome serious weaknesses and human limitations. In fact, it is the struggling that often brings us closer to God. It makes us realize how much we need God's help. The healthy thing about the bishop's talk was his ability to laugh at his handicap. It is important that we accept our limitations humbly and with humor.

The joy that radiated from these young men brought rays of sunlight into all those who came in contact with them. Children teach us how to be joyful. They find the greatest joy in the simplest things. Just being around them rekindles our own joyful childlike spirit.

Divine Spirit of Joy
　　Fill me with a joy and
　　　　enthusiasm for life;
　　Energize me with a playful spirit;
　　Give me a zest for celebrating life;
　　Teach me to delight in the innocent
　　　　who never lose
　　　　　　their sense of wonder,
　　　　but take delight in
　　　　　　the simple things.
　　　　　　　　　　Amen.

Four

Touched by Green
The Spirit of Hope

*Green, like the springtime, suffuses hope. New buds burst forth
with all the freshness of new life and new beginnings.
When days are dark, and we feel discouraged, a little touch
of green will always make a difference. Trust is believing
when all seems hopeless.*

I have always felt a tinge of sadness when autumn
comes. The happy memories of summer fade. The
leaves lose their life, flowers wither, the air grows cold, the

happy songbirds no longer stop by the feeders. Everything around me seems like it is dying or falling into a deep sleep. As children, we don't think of the spring that will be coming in a few months. We know only that everything is dying. When I was a child, my dad noticed how sad I would become as I watched the leaves fall from the trees, and even my precious daisies beginning to wither. He must have felt sorry for me because he called me over one day and said, "Dort, let's go for a walk."

We walked from the back of the house to a grove of evergreen trees near the edge of the field. Putting his arm around me, he said, "Dort, see those evergreen trees? As the leaves on the other trees fall away and die, these trees stay alive and green all through the winter. They remind us of God's love. It never changes. It is unwavering and unconditional, and ever-present. So don't ever be afraid, even when things look bleak like the winter. There is always hope of bright and cheerful things to come. Just like spring after the cold winter snow."

Looking down at me, he continued. "Dort, it is also like *my* love for you. Things around you may change, but my love for you will always be the same, ever unchanging. You may do things I do not like, but I will always love you."

Ever since that day, *green* has always given me hope and comfort during difficult times.

I never look at an evergreen tree without thinking of my

dad and of God's continual love for me. Because of the way my dad often talked to me, hope has been a powerful driving force throughout my life. What is this hope? I think it has something to do with our ability to dream, to wish that things could be better when everything looks dark and frightening. Because there's a God who cares, hope is not an unfounded fantasy, it is based on a realistic trust in God, who can make all things new and cause a bright sunny day to dawn after a dark nightmare. It is trusting a kind and loving God to fulfill a dream of accomplishing something special with our lives, even though we are so conscious of our limited talents. It is having confidence in God even when tragedy occurs, realizing like a little child that God is kind and will bring good out of this also. Hope gives us the sure knowledge that one day this loving God will bring us home to be with our loved ones forever.

God Reorganizes Our Schedule

It was a cold, blustery morning when we drove down the mountain road through the blizzard. We had left in plenty of time to catch our plane for Florida. Joseph and Mary Gamarano had invited us for the open house of Cafe Joshua, their longtime dream to help the homeless and the troubled.

Since we were scheduled to be on hand early the next morning, we had to arrive that evening.

After a seemingly endless drive through the blinding snow, we finally arrived at the airport, only to find our flight had been canceled. We waited for the next flight. That, too, was canceled, and each one after that. We were told there was an afternoon flight if we wanted to wait. It was almost noon already. The snow was piling up on the runway. What should we do? To drive back to the mountain would have been futile. To hang around the airport was depressing. We decided to drive to the nearby mall and spend the time shopping for Christmas presents. At four o'clock we called the airline office to check on the flight. We were told it had also been canceled. However, there was a flight leaving at four-thirty, but it was being delayed, so if we could be at the airport by four forty-five, they would wait for us. As we were only five minutes away, we decided to try it. We ran through the mall and out into the parking lot where our car was completely covered with snow. While Joe Girzone heated up the engine, I cleared the windows. We left the parking lot and immediately were trapped behind two slow-moving snowplows blocking the two lanes going in our direction. Our five-minute drive took us twenty-seven minutes. At four forty-three we arrived. I jumped out of the car, grabbed the luggage, and ran into the terminal while Joe tried to find a parking space in an already full lot covered with a foot of snow. Exhausted and breathless, I arrived at the ticket counter. "I'm sorry, Dorothy, the flight has been canceled." Everyone in the terminal knew us by now. Joe came running up the stairs, breathless and exasperated, only to see me half smiling. "Slow down, Joe, the flight had been canceled." We both felt helpless and discouraged. There was one flight left. It was scheduled to leave at six forty-five. We had no alternative but to wait and see.

As five-thirty approached, a tall, heavyset, boisterous gentleman in an indescribable outfit, with a kind of knit snow hat I hadn't seen in years, came strutting toward us, mumbling to himself, "I've just about had it with these damn planes, I've been here all afternoon and still no flight."

As he approached, Joe walked over to him and out of curiosity asked him his name. In a frustrating tone he replied, "Shalom, Shalom Koplowitz."

Joe said, surprised, "I know you, you are one of my brother Ed's best friends."

"Who is your brother?"

"Ed Girzone."

"I know Ed. He's a good man," he replied, then quickly added, "Oh, yeah, I know you too, you're his brother, that famous author."

"What are you doing here?" Joe asked him.

"Waiting for this damn plane. I've got to get it. My wife's

waitin' for me at the airport in Florida. Why don't you say a prayer, you're a priest."

"You're a blood relative. That's even better. You should say the prayer."

"That won't work. We have to have ten men to pray, excluding women. All you need is two or three."

"Sister Dorothy's the pray-er for airplane flights," Joe told him. "She prays them in even when the airport is closed."

"Come on, Dorothy, get over here and pray," Shalom said as he started gathering the few of us standing around.

"Hey, you there," he called to a fellow standing nearby, "you're waiting for this plane, aren't you? Come on over here and pray with us."

"I am a Jew," he said.

"So what? What's that got to do with it? Jews pray too. I'm a Jew and I pray."

"But I've never prayed in my life."

"It's about time you learned. Come on, get over here," Shalom said good-naturedly as the man walked over with a grin.

Another fellow standing nearby asked if he could join us. He turned out to be an Evangelical minister.

While all this was going on, I was talking to a lady who was also waiting for the flight. She told me that her family were Arabs from Lebanon. She asked if she could pray with us too.

I said, "Of course, that would be great."

So, there we were, standing in the middle of the terminal, the six of us, two Jews, an Arab, an Evangelical minister, a Catholic priest, and a nun holding hands and asking God to please bring this flight in so we could all get to where we were supposed to be.

No sooner had we finished the prayer than the agent called over to us, "Well, your prayers have been answered. We have just been notified your plane has been given the okay to leave Pittsburgh. It should be here in about an hour. And there won't be a problem leaving from here for Florida."

The next hour went by fast as we all spent time getting acquainted.

Though the day started out bleak, soon a rainbow of colorful events began to unfold.

We finally arrived in West Palm Beach, exhausted but relieved. Joseph and Mary, the directors of Cafe Joshua, were thrilled when we told them the story.

As I got to know this remarkable couple, I began to realize just how special they were. They had just sold an exclusive gift shop in Boca Raton, which was their livelihood, so they could fulfill a longtime dream of working with the homeless and the troubled. Most people, when they retire do not start a whole new career, they just relax and enjoy life. But not Joseph and Mary. They still had plenty of energy and enthusiasm and wanted to do something productive with their lives. Making money wasn't all there was to life, they realized. Getting to know them and seeing their rich spirituality made me realize that here was a couple who has much more to give to the homeless than just a meal.

The next morning we all gathered at the cafe. What a delightful surprise! It was not just another soup kitchen, or even just an ordinary cafe. It was a marvelous expression of ingenuity, with stainless steel stoves and ovens and ventilating hood. The walls of the kitchen were a colorful ceramic tile. The tables in the dining area were bright and cheery, decorated with fresh-cut flowers and colorful tablecloths. An internationally famous artist, Edna Hibel, donated reproductions of her paintings, which adorned the walls in the dining room.

In the kitchen, which was immaculate, was a young man busily preparing the meal for the day. I asked if there was anything I could do. He immediately gave me an apron and a job. I asked Mike where he was from and what brought him there. He told me he was from Boston, and that when he was a teenager, his parents divorced. He was left with his father, who was an alcoholic. Always alone at home, he took to the streets for companionship, where he soon became involved with drugs. Although at one point he was making well over five thousand dollars a week, his life was falling apart. One day, as the world around him was collapsing, he found himself in the street with his head bashed in. With the help of a skilled plastic surgeon, and many months in the hospital, he was completely healed. While in the hospital, a friend gave him a copy of *Joshua*. Mike told me that when he finished the book, he knew his life would never be the same.

While we were talking, the cafe was filling up with guests. The homeless dressed up for the occasion and looked sharp. You could see how proud they were by the expressions on their faces. This was their cafe, and they knew it, and it made a difference in how they felt about themselves.

By the time lunch was ready, there were over fifty people standing around socializing. In the corner of the room near the entrance, Cy Shonberg, the assistant director of the Palm Beach Opera, was playing the organ someone had donated. He came every day to provide background music while the guests were dining.

After the meal the guests moved from table to table to socialize with one another. The homeless and the well-to-do mingled with such ease, one would think they were old friends.

The next morning we spoke to a large crowd that had gathered to hear us share our "Portrait of Jesus." In the crowd were many of Mike's friends, together with a number of homeless. They came up afterward, hugged us, and thanked us for the talks we had given. I was deeply touched.

After our talk we had lunch, then drove to Mike's three halfway houses. While we were sitting around chatting, Mike said to me, "You know, there is a fellow who wanders around this neighborhood who really makes me mad. He comes around here practically every day and creates havoc. He even gives the director of the cafe trouble. He almost hit him with a street sign yesterday. I'm afraid I'm going to do something to him that I'll regret."

I suggested, "My mom always told me when someone is mean and nasty, it is because they are hurting, and if you are nice to them, it may make a difference. Why don't you give him a hug."

"Give him a hug!" he said, shocked at the suggestion. "I'll really have to think about that one."

After speaking with Mike and his friends about their dreams, pains, and how they missed their families, Mike showed us through the other two houses. The houses were desperately in need of repair, but the warmth and hospitality these young men offered us showed how far they had already come.

We spent that evening and the next morning with Mary and Joseph, and they shared with us more of their dreams, particularly about building a home for the homeless. Later that day we flew back to Albany.

Three days later, Mike called. He was so excited, he could not wait to tell me what happened.

"Sis," he said, "you won't believe this. I was looking out the window the day after you left and saw that guy walking up the street. I remembered what you told me. I grabbed a pack of cigarettes and walked out to meet him. As I approached, he looked puzzled. I reached out and handed him a pack of cigarettes and gave him a hug. He was shocked, and cried like a baby in my arms. I couldn't believe it. We are not the best of friends yet, but at least the door is open. I don't know what will come of it, but I'll keep you informed."

I was deeply moved by what Mike told me. It put a finishing touch to the heartwarming experiences of our stay in Florida. It is amazing the power each of us has to heal others just by loving and accepting them where they are at. Mike took the message of Jesus seriously and reached out and loved this man where he was at. That simple hug changed the man's life.

It reminded me of Jesus meeting the woman at the well. He knew what her life was like, married five times and now living with a man she never bothered to marry. Her lifestyle was certainly not inspiring, and yet with all the "nice" people in town, he picked her to announce the "good news." It seemed her whole life changed after that, and Jesus didn't even give her a sermon. It is amazing what can happen when we know we are loved for who we are, with all our bruises and blemishes. Most of us want to be better but don't know how to change. Loving a person back to life is a good place to start. It automatically brings the best to the surface, and then it's easy to know where to go from there. The woman at the well knew immediately what she had to do next. She had found a whole new meaning to her life because she met a man who recognized her goodness, opened up a bright new world for her. Feeling good about herself, she could travel the new road that the stranger had pointed out to her. This could be our mission too, to love in a way that helps people to recognize their inherent goodness, which others may have overlooked. Loving people where they are at helps them to appreciate themselves and encourages them to develop their latent holiness.

As I reminisced about our time in Florida, I felt that I had witnessed Jesus being reborn, a beautiful experience. Not only did I feel a new sense of hope, I could see hope in the eyes of the homeless, a hope that awakened dreams too long asleep. They had come back to life at the touch of the Master's hand.

A Friend to Children

So often today, people use circumstances in their childhood to excuse bad things they have done. Yet, here is a story of a young man who grew up under extremely difficult circumstances but who today has no trace of self-pity and was never driven to do evil things. Instead, these bitter circumstances inspired him with extraordinary hope that he could rise above his environment and find in life a remarkable adventure.

Duncan was born and raised in the inner city of Portland, Oregon. Both his parents were alcoholics who spent most of their time and money at local taverns.

In school Duncan was determined to do well. In fact, he excelled. "It was my way of making sure I would not grow up to be like my parents," he said.

Loneliness was the young boy's constant companion, but when he was old enough to explore his neighborhood, he discovered that church was a place where he could find comfort and make friends. He became active and, even though he knew little about the religion, he soon became president of the church's youth organization. He was searching for something that would help him feel good inside. During his high school and college years he was still trying to put together the pieces of life's puzzle. Having no spiritual experience as a child, he found the idea of God foreign and difficult to understand. He considered himself an agnostic. But without God the pieces of the puzzle did not make sense. It wasn't until seven years later that God became an important part of his life.

During all that time he took on several jobs to pay his way through college. On graduation, Duncan enrolled in the University of Oregon to study law.

After graduation he formed a large investment and timber management company, which gave him the resources he needed to establish his own programs for high-risk kids.

This was his real interest, helping troubled children, or children who, because of circumstances, had a high risk of getting into trouble. In order to accomplish what he wanted, he needed even more resources, so he sold his company. Proceeds from the sale made it possible to set up a substantial endowment to fund his program which he named, "Friends of the Children."

"Friends of the Children" provides an adult mentor (a *Friend*), who loves, cares, and nurtures a high-risk child all the way from first grade through high school, like a loving aunt or uncle. For Duncan, this is how Jesus would love these children if he were here today.

"Friends" are full-time paid professionals employed by

"Friends of the Children." Each "Friend" works with no more than eight children. As positive adult role models, "Friends" provide the children with the support, knowledge, skills, and attitudes they need to reach their unique potential. For many of the children, the "Friends" are the only positive influence they have, providing safety, love, and dependability in their lives. Many of them have never known what it is to feel secure and protected.

"Friends of the Children" works through fourteen Portland schools. They ask school staff to identify kindergarteners or first-graders most at risk of getting into trouble in later years or most in danger of school failure, abuse, gang involvement, teenage pregnancy, or criminal behavior. These are the ones selected for the program. If the child's family is open to the program, then the commitments last through the child's school years.

The "Friends" who work with the children are chosen after completing their applications and taking oral and written exams. Complete criminal background and reference checks are done on all applicants before hire. The focus is on one-on-one relationships. "Friends" help the children with their homework, take them to museums—stand in for their family in academic and nonacademic activities. In the process they help each child to develop his or her own interests or talents. This is the key to helping young people find the joy there is in living. Even college students need that personal attention. I found in my campus ministry that when I told the kids I needed them for a particular gift they had, their first reaction was one of surprise and then pride. "Who, me?" "Yes, you. I know you can do it. I've watched you." Then they would beam and put their whole heart into what I asked them, which was usually playing a musical instrument in the choir. Recognizing talent in a child can change the whole direction of a child's life.

"Friends of the Children" invests eleven dollars each day per child. Compared to alternatives such as juvenile detention, foster care, and drug and alcohol treatment, the program offers an affordable solution to a myriad of social needs, and at a vast saving to the community. Parents, teachers, and principals have seen improvement in the children's school performance.

Though the program is expensive, it has proven effective and is considerably cheaper than what cities and counties and states pay for juvenile lockups. Giving the children hope and a good start in life pretty well assures their healthy integration into society later on. It is the beginning that counts. Hopefully, when they succeed as adults, they may consider helping someone else.

Duncan could easily retire, relax, and enjoy life. But that is not his dream. Even if he did retire, it would only be a chance to spend more time with the children he loves. It would be a time to create other programs for children. He continues to stay focused on his goal, making this world a better place, giving hope to young people, and their parents too, to say nothing of the community at large.

Today this organization reaches over 220 children in over thirty neighborhoods. It seems God just picks certain people and, no matter how adverse their environment as children, guides them toward goals they are not even aware of, and uses them to touch the lives of countless others living on the brink of despair. Duncan seems to have been one of those chosen, unassuming, blessed souls.

Like the evergreen tree that continues to stay green through all types of weather, he never gives up on his dream of touching the hearts of children, giving them hope to believe in themselves and follow their own dreams.

Gift from God

In a rainbow, colors seem to merge. It is difficult to tell where one color ends and another begins. In the following family's tragic experience, faith, hope, and healing are so intertwined that it is difficult to tell where one heroic virtue ends and the other begins. What was clear, though, is that a new life emerged from their misfortune.

One Sunday morning while chatting with people outside church, a little boy whom I had never seen before came running out and jumped into my arms. Though a little puzzled, I was thrilled at this spontaneous show of affection and gave him a hug.

"What is your name?"

He quietly looked up at me with a smile and a pair of big brown eyes as his mother said, "He can't speak yet, but his name is Jonathan. I'm Susan."

"I'm Dorothy. How old is Jonathan?"

"He is going to be one year old next week. I'd like to apologize for Jonathan's behavior."

"Apologize? You do not have to apologize, I am thrilled that your son felt comfortable enough to come to me. He is such a happy, friendly child. What a joy he must be to you!"

"Yes, he is that all right. He is one precocious little child."

I finally let Jonathan down and Susan and her son left.

A few days later, Susan's sister-in-law called and asked if I remembered the little boy who came running up to me after church and hugged me.

"How could I forget such a child?"

"Would you pray very hard for him? The doctors are running tests on him this week. They have no idea what is wrong. He has such a happy disposition, but lately he has been crying a lot and hasn't been able to sleep."

"I promise I will pray for him every day until I hear from you."

Susan called later in the week to tell me what had happened.

"Jonathan had to have surgery on his eye. They found he has retinoblastoma. They had to remove his right eye. They also found multiple tumors in the other eye. He will have to have radiation every day for the entire summer."

I was speechless.

"Just pray they got it all. I don't know what I'll do if they don't. I cannot imagine my son blind. He is too young and full of life. I don't want this to affect his happy spirit."

Jonathan would have to have a checkup every two months for the next five years. Susan was concerned that the cancer might recur.

She had also been contemplating having another child, which the doctor strongly advised against for medical reasons.

Susan thought hard and prayed even harder for God's guidance. Her husband, Greg, was very supportive of whatever decision she might make. Deep within Susan's heart her faith gave her the courage to say, "It is in God's hands now. If I am to have another baby, that is God's decision."

Susan called me weeks later to tell me that they had decided to have another baby, hopefully a girl.

"Would you please pray for us?" she asked. "Pray that it's a girl! I love Jonathan, but I think even he would like a little sister as a companion."

A month later she called, delighted to tell me she was pregnant. I was happy for her.

All through her pregnancy we prayed. She was thrilled when the ultrasound showed that she would be having a girl. She felt blessed.

A short time before her due date her husband called early one morning to tell me he was rushing Susan to the hospital. She was bleeding profusely. I was shocked. I prayed so hard that everything would go all right. However, the baby died.

I went to the hospital to be with Susan. She was devastated. All she could say was "Why, God?"

I felt great pain as I held her lifeless baby in my arms. I gently handed the child to Susan. She held her so tenderly. I could see a sense of peace come over her. She realized that she was holding only the shell. But the child was still alive, perhaps, as a little saint in heaven.

Susan said to me, "Look, her face is shaped like a little rosebud about to blossom."

"Why don't we name her Theresa, the little flower?"

"That's an excellent idea, Dort."

The funeral service for little Theresa was touching, with the gentle words expressed that were so comforting and the expression of faith that spoke of a life of endless peace and joy.

The months that followed were extremely painful. I knew how much Susan wanted a baby girl, and she did not intend to give up the idea. Her faith was still strong even with all the odds against them having another child.

"Dort, let's pray for a healthy girl this time. I think we need to be more specific with God."

I turned to one of my favorite Bible verses, "The Spirit, too, comes to the aid of our weakness; for we do not know how to pray as we ought, but the Spirit itself intercedes with inexpressible groaning. And the one who searches hearts knows what is the intention of the Spirit, because it intercedes for the holy ones according to God's will.

"We know that all things work for good for those who love God, who are called according to his purpose" (Romans 8:26–28).

In her heart Susan knew God would listen to our prayer this time in spite of what the doctors advised. She knew that she could always count on her husband's support.

One year later she told me she was pregnant again. The next nine months were ordinary, with no complications.

She felt good all during her pregnancy. Closer to the due date I became anxious but hopeful. I finally received the phone call.

"Dort, it is a beautiful, healthy, and happy little girl! We named her Jessyca Rose."

Susan and Greg thanked God for this wonderful blessing. Their faces glowed as they looked at this lovely gift from God.

Years have passed now, and Susan continues to take Jonathan and Jessyca Rose for their yearly checkup. Each year the reports are excellent.

Jonathan is twelve now and in the seventh grade. He is still in good health. Jessyca Rose is eight and in the third grade, also in excellent health. Each day is filled with gratitude and hope as Susan and Greg see their children growing so beautifully.

I marvel at their faith: to pray against all odds, never doubting that God would answer their prayers. They believed deeply in their hearts that whatever happened was what God wanted. Some people give up their faith or lose hope through suffering; these people's faith and hope grew out of their pain and the loss of their precious little girl.

I marvel because they never expressed any anger toward God. They just asked for an explanation. I could not give them one. So often I wish I could understand the mind of God.

This experience definitely helped me grow in my faith, but it gave me the courage to trust God totally. It brought back my parents' own faith, which they tried so hard to instill in us. I grow sentimental when I remember waking up early and catching my mom sitting in the rocking chair in the living room, saying her rosary. "I give my first hour each day to God and the rest of the day I give to my family," she would say. "God must always come first."

The memory of my parents' deep faith has stuck with me all these years. Their faith was as strong and enduring as the evergreen trees they loved. I often wish I had a faith like theirs. Susan's and Greg's faith was also strong and persistent, and in the end God richly rewarded them.

When I Was Near Despair, You Gave Me Hope

It was eight-thirty Sunday morning. The musicians were hard at last-minute practice for our nine-thirty liturgy. A woman walked into the church and sat down. Even though she was a distance away, I could sense she was deeply troubled.

A parishioner arrived early and saw the woman sitting there alone. Noticing that she was a stranger, she went over to welcome her. The two women sat and talked until people began filling the church.

The stranger stayed for Mass, and left with everyone else afterward.

Weeks later, Father John, our pastor, received a letter from the woman. It read:

Two weeks ago I attended services at your church. I had a terrible fight with my husband the night before and told him I was leaving him and the four children. I drove all night, contemplating either divorce or suicide. As morning approached, I was driving up the street near your church. Seeing lights on, I knew it was open, so I went inside. I had never been to Kalamazoo, nor to your church, but I decided to stop in. As I entered I heard singing and other happy sounds, which made me feel comfortable enough to go in and sit down. After a few minutes a woman approached and sat next to me. We talked and she made me feel so much at home and so welcomed that I decided to stay. The singing, the friendliness, and love I experienced was a moving religious experience.

I decided to go back home. I sat down with my husband and children and told them how sorry I was. Things are much better now. I now have a reason to live. Thanks for saving my life.

Our team always stressed the importance of hospitality, to be aware of newcomers or anyone who looks lonely. I have often thought, you never know, you may be entertaining God or an angel in the guise of a stranger or a poor beggar.

There are numerous people who are lonely, desperate, and longing for someone to care or just listen. It takes courage to reach out and ask for help. Fortunately, this lady found someone who reached out to her in her need and gave her the confidence and hope to continue. Someone noticed and took time to listen. Sometimes people go to church to find comfort and healing. They may never notice the pain in the heart of the one sitting next to them. Just to notice and to sense others' pain is a beautiful gift. Jesus knew pain before anyone said a word and gave the hope needed to continue. This was his gift. So many of us are occupied with our own struggles, concerns, and needs that we are unaware of someone reaching out to us. It is important that we condition ourselves to be aware of others' pain, so when they do cry out, even silently, for help, we can hear them. Sometimes it may make the difference, as in this case, between life and death.

Divine Spirit of Hope,
 Make me hopeful
   in the midst of despair;
 Give me strength and tenderness
   when caring for others;
 Calm my soul
   in the midst of chaos;
 Clear my mind
   when faced with confusion;
 Keep me meek
   in offering my opinions;
 Help me strive for holiness
   when confronted with my weaknesses;
        Amen.

Five

Touched by Blue
The Spirit of Healing and
Generosity

I have always loved the color blue. Its delicate shades in the
sky, and its crystal-clear purity in a mountain lake awaken
feelings of peace in moments of solitude. The color blue
reminds me of the healing I feel when a dear friend shares
with me her dreams or beautiful thoughts of God.
I have the same feeling when I think of the goodness of special
friends who give of themselves endlessly and ask nothing
in return. I marvel at their generosity and am touched
by the selflessness of their giving.

*L*ying on a beach, watching the clouds floating overhead, the soft blue sky calms my soul. Listening to the waves as they gently wash across the sandy beach cleanses my soul. God's presence seems so close during these moments.

Once, when I was riding my bike, I came upon a beautiful blue lake that sparkled like crystal. It was so clear, I could see to the bottom. Just contemplating it brought healing and comfort. Whenever I see blue waters, a peacefulness bathes my spirit, and I want to share what I feel. Generosity, I believe, is the natural overflowing of a soul at peace.

The following stories show how the generosity of a few special people healed and enriched the lives of so many others who might otherwise have never seen a blue sky in their dismal and painful existence.

Ulster Project

Above all things, I am unable to understand how supposedly religious people can kill or maim innocent human beings, so often children, because they happen to belong to a different religion. I am confused because I cannot comprehend how they can twist their minds to think they are pleasing God, who forbids violence and murder.

Twenty years ago, an Irish Anglican priest, Reverend Kerry, visited the United States and saw how well Catholics and Protestants live together and how well their children get along. This revelation became the substance of a dream.

This dream, now called the Ulster Project, started in 1975. Each year the sponsors bring ten to twenty teens together, male and female, from the province of Ulster, in Northern Ireland. The teens stay with families in the States every summer for one month. Two of these sponsors, Betty and Gordon, became involved in the project a few years after it started. They offered their home to the students. Together with other sponsors, they planned daily activities for the visitors and their American friends. The activities were designed to establish trust between the Protestant and Catholic youth from Northern Ireland. An opportunity was provided for the young people to do things together—work, play, worship, have group discussions, and even perform community service for the poor in the area. The bonding between the teens during the month was incredible. Both American and Irish, Catholic and Protestant, became a solid, homogeneous community.

A short time later Betty and Gordon visited Ireland and found that many of the students kept up their cross-community friendships. Teens from the two segregated school's systems were dating and attending social functions at one another's school.

But things don't change overnight. A little story shows how confusing this situation still is, but points the way to hope and healing. A group of Protestant boys decided to attack a group of Catholics. Jason, who had been in the Ulster Project, was one of the gang. As they came upon a group of Catholics, they started to beat them up. Jason recognized one of the boys as a member of the project whom he had befriended. He was horrified. "Leave him alone," he screamed out, "he's my friend." This incident had a deep effect on Jason.

Many of the students, when they returned home, found it very difficult to maintain their friendships because of the pressures from family and friends. However, many of the relationships *do* survive. Another impressive fact is that so far none of the children, since they returned home, has ever been involved in subversive groups.

Reports like this one encourage Americans to continue the project. There are presently over twenty project chapters throughout the United States.

The eyes of the Irish children were opened to the heartbreaking aspects of the hate-filled atmosphere in their country. Through the Ulster Project, the teens are learning that peace will come to their country when parents stop passing on to their children their own suspicions, hatred, and prejudices.

There has been much healing as a result of this project.

Our dream is that it will continue. Our children long for a simpler and happier world. They have a right to that. We all have to expand our minds and open our hearts to those who are different.

What is happening in Northern Ireland is happening to all of us in varying degrees. Things may be a little different now, but when I was a young girl, Catholics and Protestants were forbidden to date someone of a different religion. It was difficult for me, as so many of my friends were Protestant. I liked people for who they were, for their openness and goodness, not because they went to my church. Sharon, my best friend in college, was Baptist. She had asked me to be a bridesmaid in her wedding. My parents, who were very strict about their religion, loved Sharon and recognized the absurdity of the taboos dividing friends from one another. They told me they didn't see anything wrong with my being in her wedding. She was thrilled to have me there. We are still great friends today.

On another occasion a Protestant friend was getting married. She asked me to sing at the wedding. This was also frowned upon, but I sang anyway. After the wedding a number of Protestant people approached me and said, "Your kindness in being here means so much to all of us. I think I like Catholics a little more because of you." I just smiled and continued socializing.

But things are still far from perfect. Many years later, as a campus minister, my open attitude shocked some of the more traditional clergy, especially since I welcomed people of different faiths to worship with us, and even allowed them to join the choir. Word came back to me that I should first ask them if they were Catholic. I couldn't do that. Formally joining the church was one thing, but these people did not express an interest in becoming Catholic. They just enjoyed worshiping with us because they felt accepted and at home. College students knew they were welcomed at the parish and found it was a place they could share their gifts. So we had not only Protestants but even those who said they had no faith coming to our services.

If we close our hearts to people when they are searching for God they may never find God.

Youth want to belong. Our churches need to reach out and make them feel welcomed. They will be healthier as a result. The same is true of society. Young people in prison largely have bitter feelings of rejection by parents as well as by society. It is sad that the only solution we have for these offenders is to imprison them. One can't help but wonder if, in a Christian society, we could not discover some other way to deal with criminals so God could touch these troubled souls with miracles of grace.

I believe those who have been healed of prejudice and hatred have received from God the greatest of all miracles. This kind of healing dissipates the dark clouds and opens up a vast blue cloudless sky, where, free from the frightful shackles of petty meanness, we can soar like birds toward a boundless horizon.

Hope for Youth

When Bobby married Hope, he worked in his father's bakery, delivering bread. Finding the income inadequate to support a family, he became an insurance salesman, then bought his first motel. Now he owns seven motels as well as other properties. Many people in situations like this would treasure their newfound wealth, but not Bobby. It was a chance for him and his wife to share their blessings with others. Whenever he found people in need, like the families who couldn't afford groceries, or to pay the utility bill or the mortgage payments, he reached out to help. All was done very quietly.

In the city where Bobby and Hope lived, a unique project had been under way for a number of years. It helped young people in trouble with the law. It was a shoestring operation run by a caring minister named Troy, and succeeded only because of its dedicated volunteers. Troy had a solid reputation in town for his effective approach to rehabilitating young people. A local judge was impressed with Troy's success, so he released a young man into his custody.

The judge was already predisposed to help this young man, who belonged to an influential family in town. By the end of the year the boy had changed so much, the judge felt comfortable enough to release other young men into Troy's care. After the eighteen-month program was over, those young men were emotionally strong enough to function successfully out in the community. The key factor in the rehabilitation was that they now had jobs and confidence in themselves.

At present there are fifteen young men in the program, and a number of young women in a similar program. Quite a few others have already graduated and are living productively in the community.

Both of these programs had been housed in the same facility. As time went on, and as the number of participants increased, that facility proved inadequate. At this point Bobby found a way to help. He saw what was needed and began looking for larger facilities. He found an old Catholic school for sale in the Richmond diocese. It was a solid structure. When he told the bishop about his plans and how well the program was doing, the bishop was impressed. He decided to sell the old school to him for $150,000 instead of the appraised value of $400,000. After Bobby purchased the building, he immediately turned it over to Troy's Youth Challenge Program. The building was then named Hope

Center, after Bobby's wife, Hope. The building needed extensive renovations, and the young men in the program were able to tend to those with some professional guidance. They did the painting, plumbing, tile work, and carpentry, and in the process, gained valuable experience. Within a matter of months, visitors could see a dramatic change not only in the building, but in the attitudes of the young people. They radiated a sense of pride over their accomplishments.

When I first entered the building, I felt an atmosphere of peace. From the serenity on the young men's faces, you could see God was present there.

Troy said he hopes to finish the renovation within the next six months. Their dream is to house fifty to sixty young men before the end of the year. The Presbyterian and Episcopalian churches are currently involved in the renovation. They have already renovated two buildings into living quarters and are planning to expand their work.

Many people from the city have donated items to help with the project. Carpet was donated for the entire first and second floors. Food, furniture, and equipment soon followed. The community has taken an interest and is helping in whatever way it can. The project has drawn together people of varying backgrounds, many of whom, in the past, would not have found alternatives to incarceration acceptable.

What a gift this place has been to so many. Gratitude radiates from the faces of the participants in the project because someone believed in them and gave them hope. Love is like magic, capable of changing people in ways that defy logic.

Young people often complain, "I feel lost. I would love to have a friend. I wish I could feel I belong to someone." Everyone needs a friend. We are challenged each day to reach out and befriend some lost soul.

I believe this is why so many young people today are involved in drugs and in trouble with the law. They are looking for love in places were they will only find disappointment. When we are loved and cared for, we are not driven to repulsive behavior but can handle just about anything. One of the worst evils our society faces is the feeling of abandonment among our young people. So often they feel they are in the way of their parents' happiness. Most pain is bearable, but the pain of feeling unwanted by loved ones is intolerable. That is why being hated by a community becomes attractive by comparison because at least you are not being ignored.

Results at Hope Center are graphic. In 1996 the center provided an alternative to prison for young men and women from nine different jurisdictions from Florida to Tennessee as well as from local courts.

Every bed at the Hope Center is now full. There are still many begging for its help. The center's facilities are not adequate, but it is hoping to find a way to expand.

Without the grace of God, and the faithful support and availability of Youth Challenge, as the program is called, these young people at the Hope Center would be doing over 221 years in prison. The cost, at thirty thousand per year, would be over six million dollars to the taxpayers of that community.

In addition to all the wonderful things Troy brought about for the men, at the same time he was developing a program for young women. One of the young women, Maria, was from Guam. At the time she was facing serious charges with a possible sentence of over one hundred years. When she found God in jail, a local pastor and several concerned people called Hope Center and asked for help. A real miracle took place in court. The judge released Maria and allowed her to become a resident at Hope Center. This changed her whole life.

This program has reached out to embrace troubled young people. The results are dramatic. Almost ninety percent have been successfully rehabilitated and are living productively in the community.

Young people, like all of us, need to know they can make a difference. Whenever we asked students on campus to help with community projects, they were right there, ready to travel to Appalachia, Honduras, or Mexico, to help others. In Appalachia they built and repaired homes. In Honduras we worked and played with orphaned children. In Mexico we went from village to village bringing packages of food and clothing as well as our love and playful spirit. This was so much more exciting and rewarding than many of the projects on campus. They shared not only their gifts but their hearts. There was an unspoken exchange between the students and the poor people. Even though they could not understand one another's language, they spoke to each other's hearts and left memories that will be treasured forever. Healing took place in the students as well as in the alienated poor they ministered to.

Everyone wants to make a difference of some sort in this world. If we, with our generous spirit, would reach out and touch just one soul, what a tremendous gift that would be to our world. If a delicate blue sky can be calming and healing, how much more so the warmth of a generous heart.

She Looked Like His Daughter

The train was crossing the desert on its way to Los Angeles. James was sitting in the coach looking out the window, admiring the cloudless blue sky. He overheard a young girl crying as she tried to explain to the conductor that a man had stolen her purse, which held all her money. James could see that this young girl was about the age of his own daughter. His heart went out to her. He gave her the amount she lost so that she could continue her trip.

The man sitting across from James observed it all and asked, "Why were you so generous to her?"

"Because we are all God's children. What I did I would want someone to do for my daughter, who is about the same age as that girl."

"You are like Joshua, a man I just read about in this book. He would do things like that for people. Have you read this book?"

"No, I haven't."

"I think you might like it. In fact, you can have my book. I am finished."

He took the book home and read it. He later told me: "I try to live each day the way Joshua would want me to."

A generous spirit is contagious. We never know how our actions will affect others. Each person is called to do something special for God. By design God made each of us not only important but necessary for the continuous perfecting of creation. What we do with our lives is our way of thanking God for all that has been given to us.

You Never Know When You Help a Stranger

A disabled car was parked off the road. A man was standing next to it. A young man in a pickup truck drove up and offered to help. He seemed to know just what to do and in no time at all had the stranger back on the road. Before he drove off he asked the young man his name.

"Johnny Bisgrove," he replied.

"And where do you live?"

"Auburn" was his answer.

Two weeks later Johnny received a phone call. It was from the man he had helped on the road. He said he would like to speak to Johnny in his office if he was free to come up to Rochester and meet with him.

Johnny drove to Rochester, which is about an hour away. In arriving at the office, he was warmly welcomed by the secretary.

"Mr. Eastman is expecting you, Mr. Bisgrove. He will be with you in a moment."

Mr. Eastman emerged from his office and reached out to shake Johnny's hand. Johnny recognized him, but was shocked to find him in such an elaborate office.

"Hello, Johnny! I am so glad to see you. Come into my office so we can talk."

"I'm George Eastman." (George Eastman was the president of Eastman Kodak.) "I cannot tell you how much I appreciated your stopping to help me when I was stranded on the highway. So many people passed me by that day. I had to get back to the office for an important appointment. You came just in time. I was touched by your kindness and I would like to show you my appreciation."

"That's not necessary," Johnny replied, which Mr. Eastman ignored.

"I noticed you had a little pickup truck, and I can see you are an enterprising person. How much would it take to start your own trucking business?" Johnny just sat there, stunned, not knowing what to say. After a few moments he shyly suggested a modest amount. George wrote him a check for considerably more. That was the beginning of the Red Star Express trucking company, which can now be seen on highways all across the country.

We never know whom God puts in our path each day. We should treat each person we meet with respect and dignity. I reflect on the number of times I have seen people on the highway and, out of fear, passed by. A woman has to be prudent, but can still do something. It is not only people stranded on highways who need help. People in need cross our path all day long, not necessarily in need of material things, but in need of something much more important. There are those who need friendship, or just a kind word.

There are others who need to be understood when no one seems to care. There are also people who need someone to listen when they are hurting, or a word of encouragement when things seem hopeless. Last but not least are those who need to share a joy when there is no real friend to share it with. We can easily reach out to help others, in most cases with very little effort. Often the expression of goodwill means more to the person than the help we actually give. When we meet a generous person we can't help but wish we were more giving.

Divine Spirit of Healing and Generosity,
    Heal division and tension
        in our troubled world;
    Soothe those who are
        anxious and troubled;
    Console those who
        grieve and ache.

    Make us generous and genuine
        in our relationships;
    Inspire us with a greater
        sensitivity to the poor and lonely;
    Help us to be tender yet strong
        in caring for one another;
    Purify our minds
        with a divine sensitivity.

                            Amen.

Six

Touched by Violet
The Spirit of Forgiveness

*Since I was a child the color violet always aroused in me the
feeling of sorrow, and, as I grew older, it symbolized
forgiveness. I can remember my first Lent, seeing all the
statues in church draped in violet, symbolizing sorrow for
the things we have done that hurt others deeply. It prompted
me to reflect on my own life and think of those whom I
may have offended or hurt in any way and to reach out
and ask for forgiveness.*

Almost Too Late

Ann was a theology teacher in a private school. It was Lent, and all the teachers were required to set up a program explaining to the students the importance of learning how to forgive. She began her lesson by showing a film of a modern-day parable that could have easily taken place in any home.

The story is about a father and son and the tortured relationship between them. In the first scene the two are arguing because the son, a teenager, wants to drop out of school. In anger the father lays down the law, saying, "As long as you are in this house, you will follow my rules!"

"If that's the way you feel, then I'll leave!"

"Once you go, you can never come back."

"That's fine with me," his son says as he grabs his bags and storms out the door.

In the next scene you see the boy scared and alone walking down a rainy city street. He knew he acted impetuously in leaving. He is afraid to call his father. He decides to write a letter to his mother. Would she ask his father if he could come back home? "If he will take me back, just leave a light on in the front window. If there is no light, I will keep going."

The boy was hitchhiking, and an old man picked him up. The two spent the time sharing stories. As they came closer to the boy's home, the runaway became restless because he was afraid that there would be no sign of welcome at his house. He asked the old man if there was a light in the front window.

The old man smiled. "It's all right, son, you can look."

When the boy looked, he saw not only one light but every light in the house shining brightly. He thanked the old man and jumped out of the car, running to his parents.

The students watching the film were touched by the story. "Let's talk about forgiveness," Ann said.

Immediately, somewhat boldly, one of the students asked, "Ann, is there anyone in your life whom you haven't forgiven?"

Caught off guard, she blushed. She had not spoken to her brother in six years and her father in twenty-nine years. She had never thought of applying a movie to her own life.

Taking a deep breath and swallowing her pride, she told the class the painful story. Hearing their teacher's real-life story had a much more profound effect on the students than a rather detached viewing of a story on video. Her parents divorced when she was twelve years old. It was a painful time in her life. Her father, who was an alcoholic, and abusive, had tried to kill her mother. Ann ended up living with her mother. Her brother went to live with their dad.

This hurt Ann deeply because she had always been "daddy's little girl." She found it difficult to face the fact that she might never see her father again. She made up all sorts of excuses for her dad's behavior, and kept hoping that someday they could all be together again.

Her father rarely sent child support and often jumped states so they could not reach him. She wrote to her father, but seldom heard back, except at Christmas, when he would send her money. All she really wanted from her father was his love and attention.

When she was about sixteen, her mother remarried and they moved. One day, after school, she saw a letter in her father's handwriting. She was so excited, she hurriedly opened it, never noticing that it was addressed to her mother. In the letter her father wrote: "Now that you're married, Ann is no longer my responsibility."

Ann was crushed, thinking her father no longer loved her. She threw the letter on the table and, crying, ran into the kitchen. She told her mother's new husband, "Tom, from now on I will call you my daddy." She was crushed and fed up with caring for her father, who obviously did not care for her. She decided never to write him again.

Many years later her father's third wife dropped Ann a note after her first son was born and sent a gift. Ann, still hurt and angry, sent the gift back with a letter. She wished them both well, but asked them not to contact her again.

She felt that her new daddy had earned the right to be called "Grandpop," not her father, who she had mistakenly thought no longer cared about her.

Ann's older brother, Lee, became angry about the lack of a relationship between his sister and their father, so he stopped writing and calling her. He even returned her Christmas gifts that year. After all, he felt, he still maintained his relationship with their mother. Why couldn't she do the same with their father?

Ann tried to explain to Lee what had transpired between herself and her father. He would not listen. She continued to write to her brother, but the letters were returned unopened. This hurt deeply. She had tried to make peace but there was no response. What more could she do? Though she had only one brother, he now wanted nothing to do with her.

Ann's students asked her, "Do you think you will ever be reconciled with your brother and your father?" She paused and said slowly, "Truthfully, I do not know."

Later that day, Ann told one of the other teachers what had happened in class. She said she wanted so much to be at peace with her brother, but was afraid of being rejected again. He had already returned so many letters unopened. The teacher volunteered to address the letter so that he would not recognize the handwriting.

She decided that evening to take one last chance. She

wrote and told her brother how silly it was for them to keep fighting long distance. If this was all because of her father, would he please give her their father's address so that she could write and make peace with him. She had no idea that he would ever respond, but she knew deep in her heart that it was something she had to do for herself.

Lee, who lived in Florida, happened to be in Detroit on business, and, coincidentally, not far from Ann. When he called home that night, his wife told him he received a letter from Ann. She insisted on reading it to him. "It seems that Ann is really making an effort," she said. "I really think you should give her a chance. I believe there is a reason why this letter came just before you called and while you are just down the street from her."

His wife rarely involved herself in family matters, but this time she felt it was critical. Lee listened patiently but said nothing.

At the same time as they were talking on the phone, Ann was finishing a retreat with her high school juniors. She was exhausted, and could hardly wait to get home and relax.

Driving home, she was wondering if her brother received her letter yet, and anxious as to how he would respond. As she opened the front door, she got the shock of her life. There, sitting on the sofa, was her brother Lee, talking to her husband, Larry. Larry was a gruff but gentle man, a real man's man.

"Lee, what are you doing here?"

Picking himself up out of the sofa, he said nothing, just smiled.

They both felt awkward, and did not know where to go from there.

"Your letter came today, in fact, just a few minutes ago. Julie read it to me when I called home. . . . Life's too short, Ann. I was just down the street, so I thought I'd surprise you. I was sent to Detroit on business. Quite a coincidence, isn't it?"

They reached out and hugged. "I think it's time we make peace," said Ann.

Ann's husband had been glued to the TV and was only half paying attention to what was transpiring.

"Honey," Ann said to her husband, "I think Lee and I'll go out to a restaurant and spend some quiet time together."

"That's a great idea," her husband responded without losing a moment's focus on the TV.

"Would you like to come with us, dear?"

"No, you go and have a good time." Ann might have had more luck if a commercial had been on at that moment.

They had a wonderful dinner, during which years of

healing took place. When they got back Larry was still sitting in front of the TV, snoring.

Ann and Larry took Lee to the airport. As Lee hugged his sister good-bye, he handed her a piece of paper with their father's phone number and address.

"Lee, do you think Dad will remember me? Do you think he would want to have a relationship with me? After all, it is twenty-nine years since we have spoken."

Lee was shocked. He did not realize so many years had passed. "He may be shocked at first, but I'm sure he will be happy to hear your voice. Dad has changed a lot since he's stopped drinking twenty years ago. He may not sound like the same person you remember, but I am sure he will be happy that you called. I know he still loves you."

Lee's comment was giving Ann courage. Lee reminded his sister, "You'll have to remember, Ann, that Dad had only an eighth-grade education so he finds it hard to express his feelings. You should keep that in mind when you're talking to him. I do hope you call him, Ann, because I know he would be thrilled to hear from you." They hugged, and Lee boarded the plane.

As soon as Ann arrived home from the airport, she called her dad. Dialing the phone was the hardest thing she had ever done, but she knew that she had to do it. When she heard her father's voice, she shook inside.

"Dad, this is your daughter, Ann."

At first there was a deadly silence. Her father did not think he had heard correctly, so he said, "Who?"

"It's your daughter, Ann."

Ann never forgot his response.

"Honey, I can't believe this, I have been thinking about you a lot lately. In fact, I have your picture right here in front of me. It was when you were sixteen years old."

"Dad, how come you never called or wrote to me?"

"Honey, I did not think that you could forgive me for what I did to you and your mom."

"But, Dad, that is why I am calling you, I want you to know that I do forgive you for all that has happened. Let's forget the past, I want to be at peace with you."

"Honey, you'll never know how much this means to me. I don't know what to say. It feels like a dream."

She could hear him crying. Suddenly, twenty-nine years of hurt and anger was disappearing. She felt a peacefulness she had never felt before.

Ann could not wait to tell the senior class what happened between her and her brother and father. They were touched. Some were moved to tears.

It was not over. The conversation with her father took place during Holy Week. That Easter she received a beautiful bouquet of flowers from her dad. Attached was a note which read: *To my daughter, whom I love. Thanks for not giving up on me.*

That spring her father came to visit her. They shared so many beautiful things that had taken place during those lost years. A wonderful healing took place. Can you imagine how much rejoicing must have taken place in heaven when this happened?

Ann has shared her story with many others. It has caused them to look into their own lives and make peace with estranged loved ones.

Our whole world suffers from the bitterness caused by not forgiving. People in the highest places, presidents, and heads of state are offended by hurtful comments and often form policy out of anger and spite rather than out of national welfare. Millions of dollars are spent each year by Congress as its members investigate their political enemies in an attempt to destroy them. Anger and resentment has poisoned many labor relations and made rational negotiations almost impossible. Family lives have been destroyed because of people's inability to understand loved ones' weaknesses and mistakes.

How many friendships and families have been broken because of an unintended hurt that was not forgiven? Our whole world seems to suffer from this almost universal epidemic. Somewhere along the line we have to rise above our pettiness and personal hurt and take Jesus' words seriously. "Forgive one another, or your heavenly Father will not forgive you." Children have to be taught from their earliest years not to seek revenge and to overlook the meanness of others. If we could start a movement of forgiveness with just one person, and a spirit of forgiveness took hold, a chain reaction would spread around the world, maybe even to Washington. This could alter the course of civilization in a shorter time and with a lot less energy than all the combined diplomatic efforts of the United Nations. So what are we waiting for? Let's lighten up our world with the bright color of forgiveness.

"I'm Not a Forgiving Person"

Here is a simple story of forgiveness with a different lesson to be learned.

I was scheduled to give a talk on the West Coast. A good friend, an outstanding psychiatrist, Mike, and his wife, Dorothy, picked me up at the airport.

We stopped for a bite to eat. Mike asked, "What are you planning to talk about?"

"Forgiveness."

"Excellent. Our world needs to learn to forgive more than anything. Ninety percent of my cases involve people who have been unable to forgive. They have been nursing anger and hatred all their lives. This affects their body chemistry and causes severe physical as well as mental damage. I have seen so often that once they reach out and forgive or ask for forgiveness, it is amazing how quickly they start to heal."

The next evening, after my talk on forgiveness, a couple approached me. They had just had a big fight. In fact, they were fighting all the way to the talk. The husband asked for forgiveness, but his wife refused. "I will never forgive you" were her exact words. "I don't care what you say. That's it. Leave me alone. I can't help it. I am just not a forgiving person."

They walked in and sat on opposite sides of the hall. After the talk, the wife approached me, teary-eyed, and said, "When you started talking about forgiveness, I couldn't believe it. It was as if God were speaking through you."

She started crying. Her husband approached and said, "Give it to her, Sis, she is not a very forgiving person."

"He's right, I'm not a forgiving person." Then, turning toward her husband, she said, "Honey, I'm so sorry for the way I've been. Can you possibly forgive me?"

He could see in her eyes that she meant every word. "Yes, I forgive you." Crying, they reached out and hugged each other. It was touching to witness that beautiful moment.

I never found out what happened between the two of them, nor was it important, but both of them had been deeply hurt. And yet I could tell they loved each other very much. What is it that causes such pain in people who are so much in love? I guess it is at times the difference in personalities. Someone may not be feeling well and unintentionally says things that are sarcastic, which hurt deeply. Some will nurse that hurt for a lifetime. If we are to get past these rough spots, we have to learn not to take offense at what a person says or does, especially if we know that person loves us. Usually when a person says something nasty or sarcastic, it is because the person is hurting or troubled over something. One way of handling this is to try to understand what is troubling the person. Once we realize their pain, their remarks don't hurt as much.

I have some lavender glasses, and when I set them on the table, under a fluorescent light, all the purple disappears as the glass turns a soft healing blue. When our pain is filtered through an understanding heart, peace replaces the pain.

"Tell Him I'm Sorry!"

People who work with youth will understand this short story.

Every day was an adventure when I taught eighth-graders. I never knew what to expect. I just thanked God that we got through each day. Thirteen-year-olds are so lovable, but at times so exasperating.

We usually ended the day with a prayer, and if something offensive happened during the day, they would offer a sign of peace. This one particular day there was a terrible fight on the playground. All afternoon I could tell by the look on the students' faces that they were still simmering over the incident. I had always taught them never to leave school with a grudge in their hearts. So I tried to get those involved to make peace before they went home. One of the students was adamant. "No way will I tell him I'm sorry. I don't care what you say."

"That is your choice."

That evening the boy and his mother had to go shopping in the next town. On their way they were involved in a bad accident. The boy had to be taken to the hospital in an ambulance. His mother went in the ambulance with him. "Tell him I am sorry, tell him I am sorry," he kept mumbling.

"Tell who you're sorry?" his mother asked. "What is this all about?"

"Ask Sister Dorothy, she knows."

His mother called me from the hospital.

"Sister Dorothy, could you tell me what happened at school today?"

"What do you mean?"

"I'm here in the emergency room with my son and he keeps saying, 'Tell him I'm sorry . . .' He told me you could explain what happened at school."

My heart sank when she told me what happened. I told her what happened on the playground.

"Oh, thank you, that explains it all."

The next day at school the eighth-graders came rushing in, saying, "Did you hear what happened last night?"

"Yes, I can't believe it. I was shocked when his mother called me from the hospital. What happened on the playground must have been on his mind."

A student remarked, "Well, from now on I'm not leaving school without saying I'm sorry. He was lucky. I'm telling you right now, I'm not ready to die."

It's amazing how one incident can drastically affect our lives.

Many years later this young man came to visit me. He was married by then and had three children. He shared with me how that one incident had affected his life. "Now I try never to leave the house with my wife angry, and I teach my children the importance of forgiveness and of being at peace. I don't think I'll ever forget that day. Thanks, Sis."

As I look back to my childhood, I remember a special saying my dad would repeat. "Don't let the sun go down on your anger. Life's too short to be holding grudges. Don't live with regrets." I need to reflect on the words of St. Paul: "All bitterness, fury, anger, shouting, and reviling must be removed from you, along with all malice. Be kind to one another, compassionate, forgiving one another as God has forgiven you in Christ" (Ephesians 4:31–32). I am not lovable when I am angry, I know it, but it is at those times that I need love the most. If I am holding the slightest anger, resentment, or grudge against another person, I am unable to accept God's forgiveness. Resentment in our hearts is like a block, and God's generous love cannot get past it, so we have to be willing to let go and let God forgive and heal us.

If I am angry at someone, it is very difficult to pray. My prayers lack power. Anger also affects my work and how I minister to others. It often affects my health. Suppressed hateful feelings will erupt in one way or another. The cynicism caused by smoldering anger is like a toxin that taints all our relationships, not just our relationships with those who hurt us. Even our close friends become the target of our repressed feelings as those feelings explode in ways we never intended. If our personality is to remain healthy and joyful and balanced, it is important that we learn to forgive. Forgiveness is absolutely essential to all true spirituality. When we can forgive injuries, we know our spirituality is authentic. When we come across an angry, unforgiving person, they may appear to be spiritual, but it is often a self-righteous type of spirituality, with their bitterness only lightly veiled.

Unfortunately, forgiveness is not a characteristic of many religious people, perhaps because religion has so often been associated with punishment and unforgiveness. As we can easily see, our world hungers for peace and wholeness. Until religious groups themselves learn unity through forgiveness, the secular world itself has little hope. If religious teachers can't find wholeness, how can we expect it of the secular world? Look around, read the papers, watch television, and observe people, and you will see the great need there is for forgiveness today. When Jesus says in the Scriptures "Forgive one another," he is telling us this so we can be free of the heavy burden of anger and hatred that can destroy us. Forgiving others may seem psychologically impossible, but it is the only way we will find inner peace. Forgiveness is very difficult in the beginning, and never becomes easy, but like any other virtue, it becomes less burdensome with practice and, in time, is just a part of our ordinary way of doing things.

Painful things are very much a part of everyone's life. Some people's lives are enriched by their hardships. Other persons' lives sour through their hardships. But hurt caused by others can be a source of great spiritual growth if we approach it with faith and wisdom.

Usually when someone is mean or nasty, it is because they are hurting. We need to look at others with the understanding eyes of Jesus, with eyes that see so clearly, that can feel the pain and understand the problems and pressures that trigger hurtful behavior. If we want to grow spiritually and have that inner peace, we have to reach out and forgive. Only then can we attain the peace that opens the channel through which the voice of God can speak to our hearts.

Like the light filtered the colors in the lavender glass, turning it to peaceful blue, if we allow the light of God's understanding to filter through the purple shadows of our hurt, we will find the quiet peace that only God's love can give.

Divine Spirit of Forgiveness,
 Heal me of
  hurtful memories;
 Help me to understand so
  I won't be quick to take offense;
 Humble me enough to
  admit my weakness;
 Increase my vision to
  see pain and oppression in others;
 Transform me
  into the person I am to become;
 Forgive me
  for being impatient
  for being cynical
  for discounting others
  for narrowness of mind
  and smallness of heart

        Amen.

Seven

Touched by White
The Spirit of Wisdom

White is the essence of all the colors.
We see this dramatically in a rainbow.
As the white rays of the sun are dispersed through the drops
of falling rain the component colors of the sun are separated
and appear as a rainbow in the sky. Although the rainbow
appears to be an arc, it is really a circle and the sun is always
at a point opposite the center of the rainbow.
White symbolizes the spirit of wisdom, the wisdom that comes
from experience and knowledge. It is like the voice of God
within that leads us to places unknown, and stretches

*us beyond the limits with which we have always felt so
comfortable. It challenges us to reflect on who we are, what we
are about, and where we are going. That spirit prods us to take
notice and listen to the inner voice that beckons us to follow.*

I have for many years felt like the whirlwind. My family called me the "white tornado." I was always busy
either organizing, rearranging, or helping someone. I always
felt the busier I was, the more pleasing my life would be to
God. As deep as was my faith and my attachment to God, I
still felt a strong need to be a Martha, although I seem to
have accomplished most when I was just listening.

I never thought I had enough time for solitude. I was
always on the run. I guess I was afraid to be quiet and to
listen to the voice of the Spirit. It can be frightening. We
get to know too much about ourselves when we are quiet.

These words, "Be still, and know that I am your God!" at
times haunted me. But an inner voice kept saying, "Be still,
Dort, be still!" I was afraid to be still. To be still means to be
silent, and if we move the letters around it can spell *listen.*
Only when I am silent will I hear what God is calling me to.

It is amazing how we can change. My personality had
been for years totally outgoing. Now that my ministry has
changed, I am surprised at how quiet and peaceful I have
become. I never thought I would be able to write. I never sat

long enough to write anything more than a few paragraphs to my friends, but each situation we are in brings forth another facet of our personality that may not have been developed when we were on the run.

We become wiser from experiences. I believe wisdom is born in the heart, a heart at peace. I remember my parents saying to one of my sisters, "When you get your head and heart together, you will make wise decisions."

I may grow intellectually and experience many things in my life, but unless the external sinks deep within my heart, it cannot move me or even help me discover what I am capable of becoming. After reading the Book of Wisdom, I have chosen wisdom as my daily companion. Wisdom, the spirit of God, helps me better understand the wonder of God and God's son as my ever-faithful love. I like to look at Wisdom, the Holy Spirit, as the feminine side of God.

Why Us, God?

A number of years ago a child was born to a very wealthy couple who were deeply in love. The doctor came from the delivery room with a frightful look. Andrew knew immediately that something was wrong.

"What is it, Doctor? You look horrible."

"Andrew, it is so difficult to tell you this. The child is a boy, but he has only stumps for arms and legs."

Both the doctor and the father broke down and cried in each other's arms uncontrollably.

"What should we do?" the father asked. "Does Marianna know it yet?"

"No, I just couldn't get myself to tell her."

"What should we do?"

"Well, no one else knows about it. We could say the baby was stillborn and we could dispose of it. No one would know the difference. I don't know if you could feel comfortable with that. The baby will be totally helpless, and will need twenty-four-hours-a-day attention. His life will never be productive."

"No, no, no, no, I could never do that. My faith tells me that God has a reason. I can learn to accept it, with God's help. I have long learned that God is beautiful, but just sometimes so difficult to understand. In time we learn to see God's purposes unfold."

When they finally told the mother, she was beside herself. It took the longest time for the couple to resign themselves to what appeared to be a terrible tragedy. They knew the rest of their lives would never be the same.

Being wealthy, they were able to hire attendants to help care for the child. Through this painfully humbling experience, the parents' faith and courage grew stronger with every passing day. It also tested their commitment to each other. They remained steadfast and loyal to each other.

As time went on, Marianna hired tutors to teach her son to read and to tell him stories. Bernard had a prodigious memory. He never forgot a thing. Even as a child he had a curiosity and thirst to learn everything he could. He was forever questioning his tutors about whatever would cross his mind.

When he was hardly ten years old his teachers had already read hundreds of books to him. Noticing that family guests often spoke different languages, he was determined to understand them. His mother had special teachers brought to their house to teach him languages.

When children in the neighborhood found out about Bernard's brilliance, even though they had never visited him before, they now came and asked if he would help with their assignments in school. This continued right through the children's college years.

When Bernard was in his early twenties grown-ups began coming to him with their problems. Calmly, and with uncanny wisdom, he would probe their confusion and pain and point out to them the cause of their problems, and offer suggestions that might help. People wondered where this young man found such wisdom, when he never left the family's estate and never went to school. Politicians, judges, lawyers, and highly placed government officials came from miles around to ask his advice and counsel on the most complex matters of state, science, and philosophy. Even theologians could not help but admire the depth of this young man's spirituality. Although he never had the ability to heal people's bodies, those he healed in spirit could be numbered in the thousands.

Bernard was still a young man when he died. Few people who were whole in body and with a longer lifespan have ever accomplished as much or affected the lives of so many as this young man, whose life so many had predicted would be useless and a waste.

It is difficult to know what God has in mind for each of us. We are not aware of our purpose or the effect we may have on others when we are being simply ourselves. In our silent manner we simply respond to the Spirit within us. It is this divine Spirit that uses us to accomplish daily miracles in the lives of those around us. It is God living in us and through us as we touch each other's lives and continue enriching God's creation.

A Dozen Unexpected Blessings

Margaret Campbell was a delicate child, more so after her attack of scarlet fever, which left her heart and other internal organs severely damaged. Her doctor, who had taken care of her from birth, and who was like a father to her, strongly advised her never to marry, telling her it was medically impossible for her to have a child and survive. However, Margaret had her own dreams and a deep faith, and decided she wanted to marry. She met a young Italian immigrant who fell deeply in love with her. Although at first he was not particularly religious, Margaret inspired him with her own faith and love and they soon married. Not long afterward, she became pregnant. At her next visit to the doctor, he became deeply troubled. He felt certain she would not survive, and insisted she have an abortion. It was entirely too risky for her to continue the pregnancy. Even though she loved the doctor and respected him, her own deep faith convinced her that she would not only survive, but would have a beautiful baby. Reluctantly, she left her doctor and went to another doctor, telling him she wanted to have the child no matter what might happen to her.

Months later the child was born, strong and healthy. Margaret was ill for weeks afterward, but she recuperated. This little child that had caused so much soul-searching and concern was now her greatest joy and comfort, though he was a ball of energy. Once he learned to walk, she could not keep him down. Closing off the backyard so he would have room to run around, she found that not even this could contain him. He found loose boards in the fence and would disappear. But she was glad he was so healthy. As much as the little tyke drained her energy, Margaret and her husband loved children and decided to have as many as they could. After their fifth healthy child, Margaret met her old doctor while shopping one day. It was a tearful meeting. They were happy to see each other. "Margaret, it is so good to see you. It has been so long! How is your son?"

"Good, Doctor, and so are the other four."

"You mean to tell me you have five children?"

"Yes, Doctor, all well and healthy, thank God."

"Well, Margaret, I never believed in God, but if you have five children, I'll tell you right now, there has to be a God. Why don't you come up to my office someday for old time's sake?"

A short time later she visited his office. As she entered, she noticed on the wall a plaque with a prayer on it entitled, "A Doctor's Prayer to God," in which the doctor spoke of his former disbelief that turned into a profound faith after witnessing occurrences his medical mind thought impossible.

But that is not the end of the story. Margaret and her husband, Peter, went on to have seven more children, though her health continued to be fragile. This beautiful couple had a faith that was undaunted. After the last child, Margaret became seriously ill. The doctor did all he could, but her heart and her body were too weak, and one night the doctor called Peter to tell him his wife was dying, assuring him they had done all they could to keep her alive.

"Thank you, Doctor, but she will be all right. Her job is not yet done. God has a lot more for her to do."

"Peter, I don't think you understood me. Margaret is dying. She probably won't last another half hour."

"I know what you said, Doctor, but she'll be all right. Her job is not yet done."

The doctor hung up, a little annoyed. Peter called the kids out of bed. "Let's all come into the parlor and say the rosary together. We have to pray that God will give us your mother back."

As soon as they finished the last prayer, the phone rang. It was the doctor. "Peter," he said, "I really don't know how to tell you this, but your wife did die. However, something strange happened. When she died, we turned off the oxygen, pulled out the needles, and pulled the sheet over her head. We then left the room. The nurse had forgotten something and went back to get it. I heard some commotion, so I went back into the room and was stunned to see your wife sitting up in bed with the sheet over her head. It was a shock! We removed the sheet and I examined your wife. And I can tell you, Peter, if your wife is as well tomorrow as she is today, there is no reason she can't go home in the next day or two."

Margaret lived for some thirty years after that, long

enough to see and enjoy her twenty-seven grandchildren. Although only a privileged few may have known Margaret and Peter, there are millions who know their first child, Father Joseph Girzone, the author of *Joshua*.

In our age of science and sophistication we have been taught to trust only tangible facts. Living on faith and trusting in the unknown, even though the unknown may be God, is foreign to our "advanced" way of thinking. We are inclined to relegate spirituality and things of faith to the uneducated. We smile at people who have deep faith and are almost tempted to ask them how much of an education they had. When we come across a couple like Peter and Margaret, we wonder if perhaps it is not we who are educated beyond what our intelligence can handle, and have lost our sense of reality.

Margaret's and Peter's lives force us to reconsider that maybe we are the ones who have missed something in our education. Maybe there is a world beyond the senses and a God we never took too seriously. Maybe this world of faith and a life lived in the spirit does make sense after all.

Peter was in many ways a simple man. He never went past the sixth grade, and worked as a meat cutter all his life. In spite of that simplicity, people with education far beyond his—judges, doctors and lawyers, newspaper publishers and editors, and Ph.D.s in science—would come into his store after hours and share with him their pain and their personal problems and ask for his advice. It was almost like a private club in which they all came to know one another and would joke about how dependent they were on this simple man's wisdom. It makes one realize that the wisdom that comes from God has more value than a college degree in teaching us how to live and cope with life's complexities.

Our advanced society glorifies learning through the senses and holds as suspect the wisdom that comes from faith and intimacy with God. The highly educated people who came to visit that simple man in the evenings had found their learning inadequate to resolve life's problems.

Our inner spirit of wisdom helps us discern what is good and holy. True wisdom is seeing the essence of God in *all* its manifestations. It is the ability to interpret God to those who are searching for God. The mystery of God is God's unfathomable love for all of us.

Divine Spirit of Wisdom,

We praise and thank you
    for speaking to us in ways we least expect.
You loved us
    when we felt unlovable;
You gave us courage
    when our fears overwhelmed us;
You brought joy and enthusiasm to our soul
    when we were stricken with sadness;
You filled us with hope
    when we were ready to give up;
You healed our minds
    when we experienced hurtful memories;
You forgave us for being angry
    when our hearts were filled with resentment.

Spirit of wisdom, we ask you to help us to be wise
in making choices and forgive us for not always
being true to your ideal for us. Heal our minds
and hearts with your love and grace, and fashion
us in your image.

                                                    Amen.

Epilogue

*I*sn't it delightful to meet people whose love encourages us to take risks? The stories I have related in this volume are living examples of people who in some way were touched by the Spirit, took risks, and found that their risks paid high dividends, not just for themselves, but for the many lives they touched. Their risks made a great difference in the future of thousands of people, some of whom they may never meet. Scanning the lives of these people and how their care and courage affected the larger community, I cannot help but wonder what our world would be like if each person touched just one other person's life in a positive way.

We all want to make a difference, but often we do not know how to. Opening our lives to God is a good beginning. Having done that, occasions will present themselves in ways we never dreamed. Starting can be the greatest hurdle, but once we've begun, we lose our fear. Once we accept the risk, things just seem to happen. All God needs is our goodwill and our generous response. When we offer that with sincerity, occasions to accomplish things just seem to pop up out of nowhere. It may be a phone call from someone requesting help or advice. It may be an event we just happen to come upon, or a meeting we attend. Opportunity often comes from the most unexpected sources. But from that day on we are well on the way, often, into the greatest adventure of our lives. We then become the Hands and Heart of God as God reaches out to others through us. Isn't that what life is all about? God has given each of us a special gift, the ability to touch the lives of others. When we open our hearts to God, from that moment on the Divine Spirit uses us in ways we could never have imagined.

As God set the rainbow in the sky to mark his covenant with Noah, so God places a rainbow in each of our lives, offering us a covenant of friendship. It is up to each of us to respond to that offer. We can either ignore it, reject it, or embrace it. It usually takes many years before we appreciate what God is offering us, but when we do, and when we respond to God's love, the rainbow comes to life and manifests itself in a living kaleidoscope of color. Everything, even the simplest of events, has new meaning. Love, courage, joy, hope, healing and generosity, forgiveness, and wisdom each takes on a color and a meaning it never had before. Our whole life from then on becomes a fascinating adventure with God.